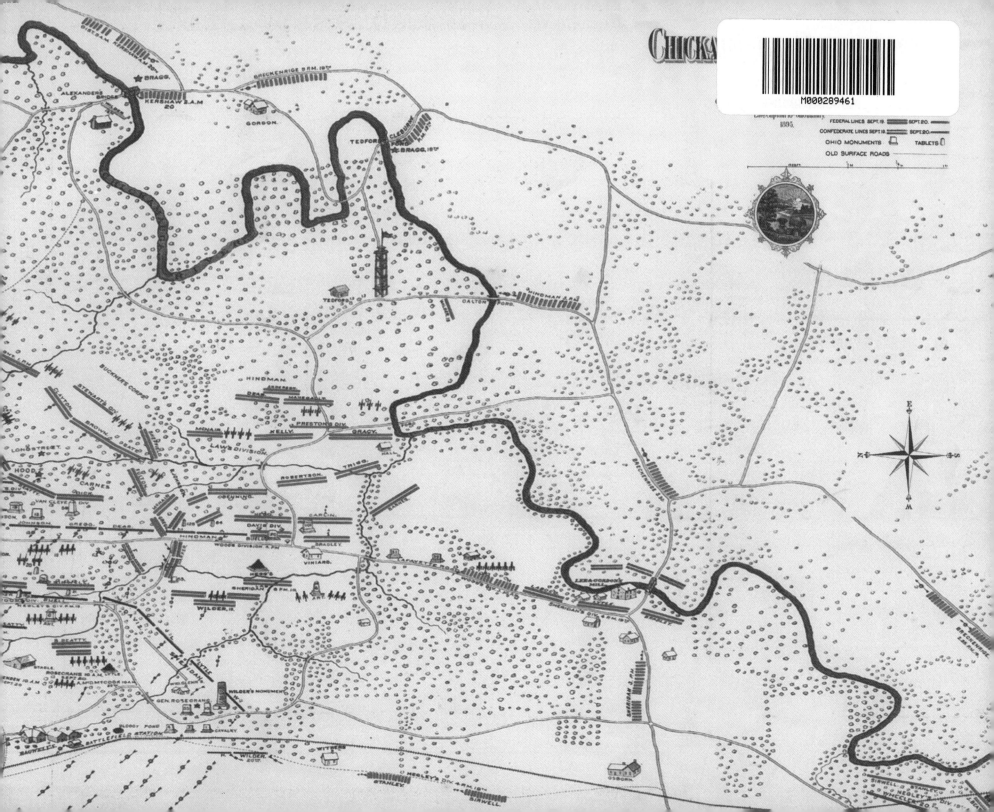

The Second Georgia Infantry Regiment

1861-1865

THE 2ND GEORGIA INFANTRY REGIMENT WAS ORGANIZED IN APRIL 1861 AND COMPOSED OF COMPANIES RAISED IN THE COUNTIES OF BANKS, MERIWETHER, MUSCOGEE, BURKE, FANNIN, CHEROKEE, WHITFIELD, MARION, AND STEWART. From April, 1862, until April 1865, it served in General Toombs' and later General Benning's brigade, known as the Rock Brigade comprised of the 2nd, 15th, 17th and 20th Georgia Infantry Regiments. It fought with the Army of Northern Virginia except when it was detached with Longstreet at Suffolk, Chicamauga, and Knoxville. The 2nd was also involved in the Petersburg siege south of the James River. At the time of its surrender at Appomattox there were just 12 officers and 146 men present.

Company D, known as the Burke Sharpshooters, was the color company of the regiment. The battle flag used by the regiment was as shown here until such time as the Confederate battle flag was adopted for use and this flag returned to Waynesboro, Georgia.

Indigo Custom Publishing

Publisher	Henry S. Beers
Editor-in-Chief	Joni Woolf
Designer	Julianne Gleaton
Assistant Designer	Daniel Emerson
Operations Manager	Gary Pulliam
Associate Publisher	Richard J. Hutto
Executive Vice President	Robert G. Aldrich

Printed in Hong Kong

Library of Congress Control Number: 2005920074

ISBN:0976287536

Henchard Press, Ltd

Indigo Custom Publishing, LLC

Indigo custom books are available at quantity discounts
with bulk purchase for educational, business, or sales promotional use.
For information, please write to:
Indigo Custom Publishing, 3920 Ridge Avenue, Macon, GA 31210, or call 866-311-9578.
www.indigopublishing.us

Acknowledgments

IN RESEARCHING THIS BOOK, IT HAS BEEN MY PRIVILEGE TO CONSULT WITH SPECIAL PERSONS, AND HAVE THEM SHARE WITH ME, DOCUMENTS, MATERIALS AND OTHER ITEMS OF HISTORICAL SIGNIFICANCE, PARTICULARLY BROTHERS PAUL AND ROWLAND DYE OF WAYNESBORO, GA; MR. AND MRS. J. MILLER BYNE OF CHARLOTTE, NC AND WAVERLY PLANTATION, WAYNESBORO, GA; J. WALKER HARPER (1916-2000) AND JAMES E. BLANCHARD OF AUGUSTA, GA, who had the foresight to transcribe and deposit the civil war diary of his grandfather and great grandfather respectively; James E. Harper with the Richmond County Historical Society; Charles E. Rowland IV, who transcribed the journals of Catherine Barnes Whitehead Rowland; and Gratton W. Rowland for preservation by photocopying and binding same. Also, the staff of the following public and private entities: Appomattox Courthouse National Historic Park; Richmond National Battlefield Park; Fredericksburg-Spotsylvania National Military Park; Manassas National Battlefield; Gettysburg National Battlefield Park; Chickamauga-Chattanooga National Park; Antietam National Battlefield; The National Archives, The Library of Congress, The Museum of the Confederacy, Richmond, VA; The Rabun County Public Library, Clayton, GA; Historic Augusta, Inc., The Augusta Museum of History, and The Augusta Genealogical Society, all of Augusta, GA; The Longstreet Society, Gainesville, GA; and The True Citizen Newspaper, Waynesboro, GA.

Also, those descendants of William Harper (1794-1857) and his wife Mary Ann Cashin Harper (1806-1854), parents of , inter alia, brothers Henry Clay and James E. Harper, of Augusta, GA; who, over the years, so freely shared their knowledge of family history, ideas and enthusiastic support for the publication of this book and John Webb Howard (1870-1945) who, in 1939, prepared the Harper Family Chart for the period 1604-1939, a copy of which is located in the Adamson Library of the Augusta Genealogical Society in Augusta Georgia.

I also thank Henry, Rick, Gary, Joni, Julianne, Daniel and the entire staff of Indigo Custom Publishing, of Macon, GA for their patience, cooperation and belief in the worthiness of this publication.

I thank Madeline McNair Harper for her encouragement, and our grandchildren Graham Harper Hill, Madeline Katherine Hill, Robert Lawton Harper, Luke Whetsell Harper, Henry Phillips Harper and Katherine McRae Harper for their inspiration.

I especially thank my wife, Sharon Parker Harper, who, by her support, assistance and commitment, enabled this publication to become a reality.

F. Mikell Harper
Rabun Gap, Georgia
Spring 2005

Table Of Contents

Foreword

IN AUGUST 1863, ONE MONTH AFTER GETTYSBURG, MY GREAT-GREAT-GRANDMOTHER, EMMA EVE LONGSTREET, WROTE TO JAMES TO TELL HIM OF HER NEW SON'S BIRTH AND TO ASK APPROVAL TO NAME THE BOY FOR HIM. James responded from the battlefield that he would be honored. Thus began what is now four generations of his namesakes.

As a child I was there when James' widow, Helen Dortch Longstreet, unveiled a memorial near his birthplace at Edgefield, South Carolina. The very fact that the widow of a Confederate general was still active in my childhood (she was a riveter on B-29s in the Second World War!) shows just how little time has actually passed since our Civil War. I was a student at Georgia Tech when I attended her funeral in Atlanta in 1962, and by that time the city had already resurrected itself as the modern hub of the South.

James Longstreet was the consummate warrior, tenacious and unyielding, who seized his foe by the throat and did not let go. He was a brilliant tactician who did not engage the enemy indiscriminately, but rather he maneuvered his foe to the place that was most to James' ultimate advantage. He led by example, being always at the head of his men leading them rather than staying safely behind while ordering them into battle. He shared the daily danger of war with his men; he loved them and they loved him. They spoke with pride of being in "Longstreet's Corps."

James Longstreet was a passionate Confederate, but when the South's military defeat became a harsh reality he saw clearly that the South's only hope for the future was to accept the victor's terms, rebuild the nation and once again enter fully into the national political and social discourse. He became a strong advocate for reunification, with full civil rights and equal treatment under law for everyone. He became just as passionate an American as he had been a Confederate, and for that many would never forgive him.

Mikell Harper has restored life to the voices of some of the men who fought alongside General James Longstreet, as well as the families they left behind. His book, *The Second Georgia Infantry Regiment*, has an immediacy that speaks across time, telling of friendship, loyalty and sacrifice – both on the battlefield and at home. Many are the books that speak of or for others; few are the books that allow the people to speak for themselves. These published diaries do exactly that and from these pages appear old names, old friends, and places, seen in a new light.

James Longstreet Sibley Jennings, Jr.

These Few...This Band Of Brothers

FROM THE RED HILLS OF
GEORGIA THEY CAME, TO
MANASSAS AND ANTIETAM, TO
FREDERICKSBURG AND GETTYSBURG;
FROM THE WILDERNESS CAMPAIGN AND
SPOTSYLVANIA TO PETERSBURG, THEY
FOUGHT ON, EVEN AS THEIR NUMBERS
DWINDLED AND THEIR SUPPLIES
EVAPORATED. Many native sons—men of the
2nd Georgia Infantry Regiment—died on distant
battlefields. But some returned, bringing their diaries
with them, an unembellished accounting of the glory
and hell that is war. This, then, is part of the record
of those men—and the women they left behind—
and their deeds.

In spite of how grand and expansive the conflict
may be, war is always personal, and never more
personal than in that dark time in this nation's
history when brother took up arms against brother
in the great American Civil War. The same men who
exchanged pleasantries as they walked pickets by
night, fixed their bayonets and loaded their rifles in
the morning light, intent on killing each other.
A Confederate soldier would give water from his own
canteen to a dying Yankee—one he may have just
shot.

Underneath the blue and gray uniforms of
competing armies were blood brothers and cousins
of a nation now divided. From every part of this
great land, men took up arms to fight for what they
believed was a great cause. And they killed each
other in record numbers: more Americans died in the
Civil War than in any other war in history.

This record of the 2nd Georgia Infantry
Regiment tells the stories of a few of the players on
the great stage of that bitter war; in their own words,
men and women from across Georgia recorded the
fears and hopes of their people, of the deprivation
and loss as the war wore on, of the courage and
endurance and passion of a people who were certain
that God would bring them victory in the end. It is
the story of their capacity to bear the unimaginable
with heads held high and dignity intact while they
buried their dead, cared for their wounded, and
tried to hold on to remnants of a way of life that was
disappearing before their very eyes. Their stories are
the stories of every man who ever marched off to an
uncertain future, in a war whose cause they might
not fully comprehend. But they believed fiercely
in doing one's duty, and saw this as theirs. So they
went.

Here are the diaries of real people who had a
sense of history, an understanding of the importance
of writing down both ordinary and significant events.
In so doing, they have provided extraordinary insight
into the everyday-ness of the conflict. Their voices
tell the stories of courage, gallantry, tragedy and
ultimately defeat—and finally, the will to get on with
life, as Americans all.

A history of the Burke Sharpshooters was written by Mrs. Lucy A. Blount, entitled The Complete History of this Gallant Company and published in the True Citizen, April 26, 1902. Her complete account follows and we are told:

THE BURKE SHARPSHOOTERS, A COMPANY COMPOSED OF THE FLOWER OF MANHOOD, DONNED THE CONFEDERATE GRAY AND WERE FULLY EQUIPPED AWAITING THEIR COUNTRY'S CALL. How little did they think when leaving Waynesboro on April 19, 1861, amid cheers and tears, of the long weary months and the disastrous end before them, for war by hearsay and war in reality are two very different things. Experience alone reveals what it is - the horror, the sorrow, the agony and heartache.

The Sharpshooters were commanded by the following commissioned officers: Captain William R. Holmes; 1st Lt. J.P.C. Whitehead; 2nd Lt. R.H. Oakman; 1st Sergeant H.H. Perry; Color Sergeant W.D. Whitehead.

From Waynesboro they went to Savannah where they were quartered in a warehouse for three days. From thence they were taken on the steamer "Habersham" to Tybee. After camping six weeks in the Island they were ordered to Brunswick.

At this time the 2nd Georgia Regiment was organized. The Sharpshooters was the Color Company and known in the regiment as Company D. The officers of the Regiment were Col. Paul J. Semmes of Columbus; Lt. Col. Skid Harris of Cherokee County; Maj. E.M. Butts of Marion County.

While here measles broke out among the soldiers and Company D lost two men. Enock Perkins was sent home and died. William Harold died in camp and was buried with military honors.

Tybee Island Lighthouse-1861

(Confederate.)

14 | 2 | Ga.

H. Harper

Pvt , Co. D , 2 Reg't Georgia Infantry.

Appears on

Company Muster Roll

of the organization named above.

for 19 April to 30 June, 1861.

Enlisted:

When 28 May, 186

Where Tybee Island

By whom W. R. Holmes

Period

Last paid:

By whom

To what time 186

Present or absent Present

Remarks:

Book mark:

(842)

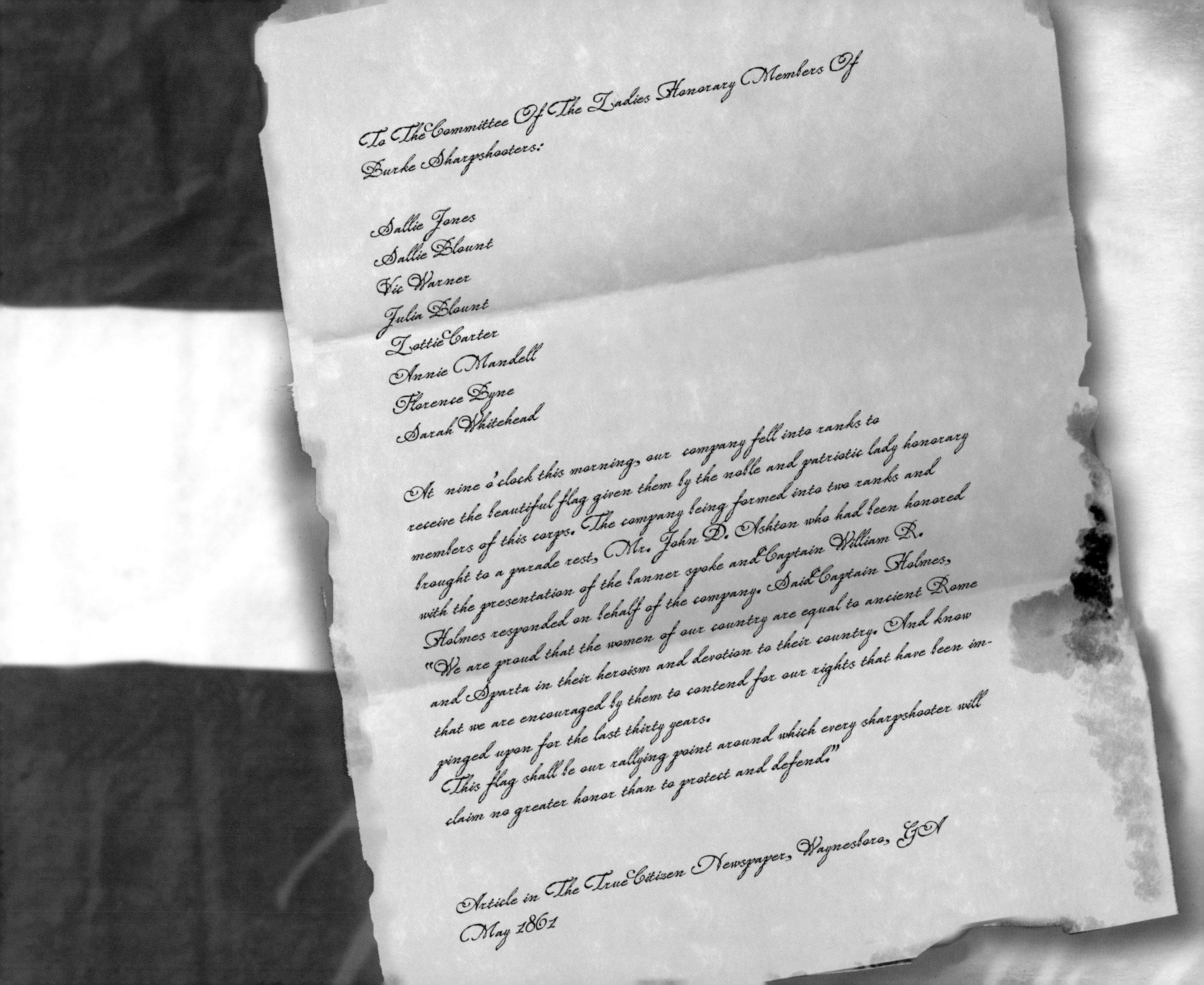

To The Committee Of The Ladies Honorary Members Of
Burke Sharpshooters:

Sallie Jones

Sallie Blount

Vic Warner

Julia Blount

Lottie Carter

Annie Mandell

Florence Byne

Sarah Whitehead

At nine o'clock this morning, our company fell into ranks to receive the beautiful flag given them by the noble and patriotic lady honorary members of this corps. The company being formed into two ranks and brought to a parade rest, Mr. John D. Ashton who had been honored with the presentation of the banner spoke and Captain William R. Holmes responded on behalf of the company. Said Captain Holmes, "We are proud that the women of our country are equal to ancient Rome and Sparta in their heroism and devotion to their country. And know that we are encouraged by them to contend for our rights that have been im-pinged upon for the last thirty years.

This flag shall be our rallying point around which every sharpshooter will claim no greater honor than to protect and defend."

Article in The True Citizen Newspaper, Waynesboro, GA

May 1861

I N AUGUST 1861, THEY LEFT BRUNSWICK AND WENT TO RICHMOND, VA. FROM RICHMOND THEY MARCHED TO CAMP WYNDER, REMAINING TEN DAYS BEFORE GOING TO OCQUIC CREEK. From here they continued their march to Manassas where they camped for ten days. We next find them at Centreville where they were assailed by the maladies of war in the dreaded enemy; death stared them in the face, in the strife of typhoid and camp fever. Fortunately, however, Company D lost but one man, W.L. McElmurray.

In April 1862, they were ordered to Richmond. From here they went by steamer to Yorktown and here for the first time they were under fire. A North Carolina regiment was run out of trenches at dam No. 1 and the second Georgia was ordered to reinforce them. They were entrenched for twenty days, being relieved every twenty-four hours. They fully realized that within the trenches they defended their safety, for the rapid and continued firing of the Federal Sharp Shooters made it impossible for a man to raise his head to view. In this encounter Burke County lost its first blood, caused by a wound received by Stephen Blount. William Skinner also received a wound from which he died at a Richmond hospital, where he had been sent.

While at Yorktown the regiment reorganized for three years of war, Captain William R. Holmes being made Lieut-Colonel; Walter A. Thompson, Captain; W. H. Dickinson, 1st. Lieutenant; J. C. Sapp, 2nd. Lieutenant; H. H. Perry, 3rd. Lieutenant; and J. W. Reynolds, Sergeant.

Camp Georgia
Winter Quarters 1861-1862

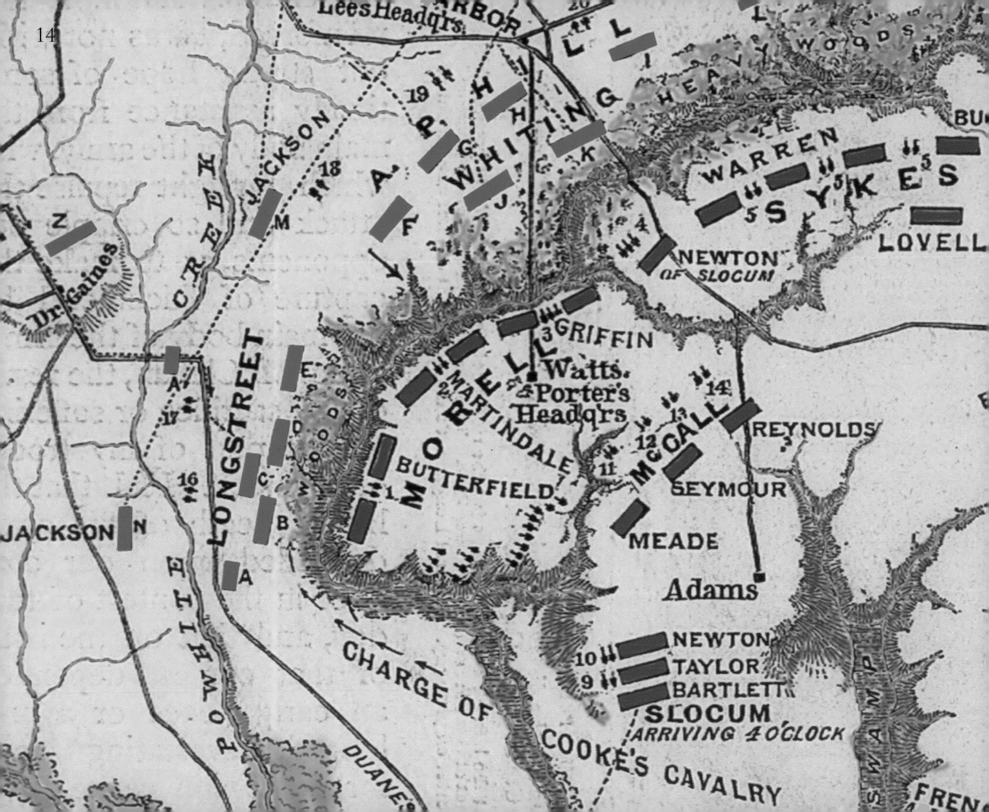

Seven Days

JUNE 26 – JULY 2, 1862

WHEN MAGRUDER EVACUATED YORKTOWN, THIS REGIMENT LEFT FOR RICHMOND, AND ON THE WAY TO THAT CITY CRAWFORD LOVETT WAS SUDDENLY SEIZED WITH ILLNESS AND HAD TO BE LEFT WITH A FAMILY ON THE ROADSIDE. IT WAS SUPPOSED THAT HE DIED, AS NOTHING WAS EVER HEARD FROM HIM. W. M. Rhind was also taken sick and sent to Richmond, where he died. The regiment remained in Richmond until June 26, 1862, engaging in picket duty. Then followed the Seven Days fight, beginning about two hours before sunset on the 26th. In this engagement the men wounded of Co. D. were H. H. Perry, S. W. Blount, R. H. Chandler; died - Tarver and Sol Parker. The next fight occurred at Savage Station. There were no casualties. On July 1st the battle of Malvern Hill was fought. In this fight Capt. Walter A. Thompson and W. D. Whitehead were killed. J. P. Sawyer, Thomas E. Blount, H. C. Harper and J. W. Reynolds were wounded. The vacancy caused by the death of Capt. Thompson was filled by Lt. Dickinson. J. P. Sapp was made First Lieutenant, H. H. Perry second, and D. W. Packard, third.

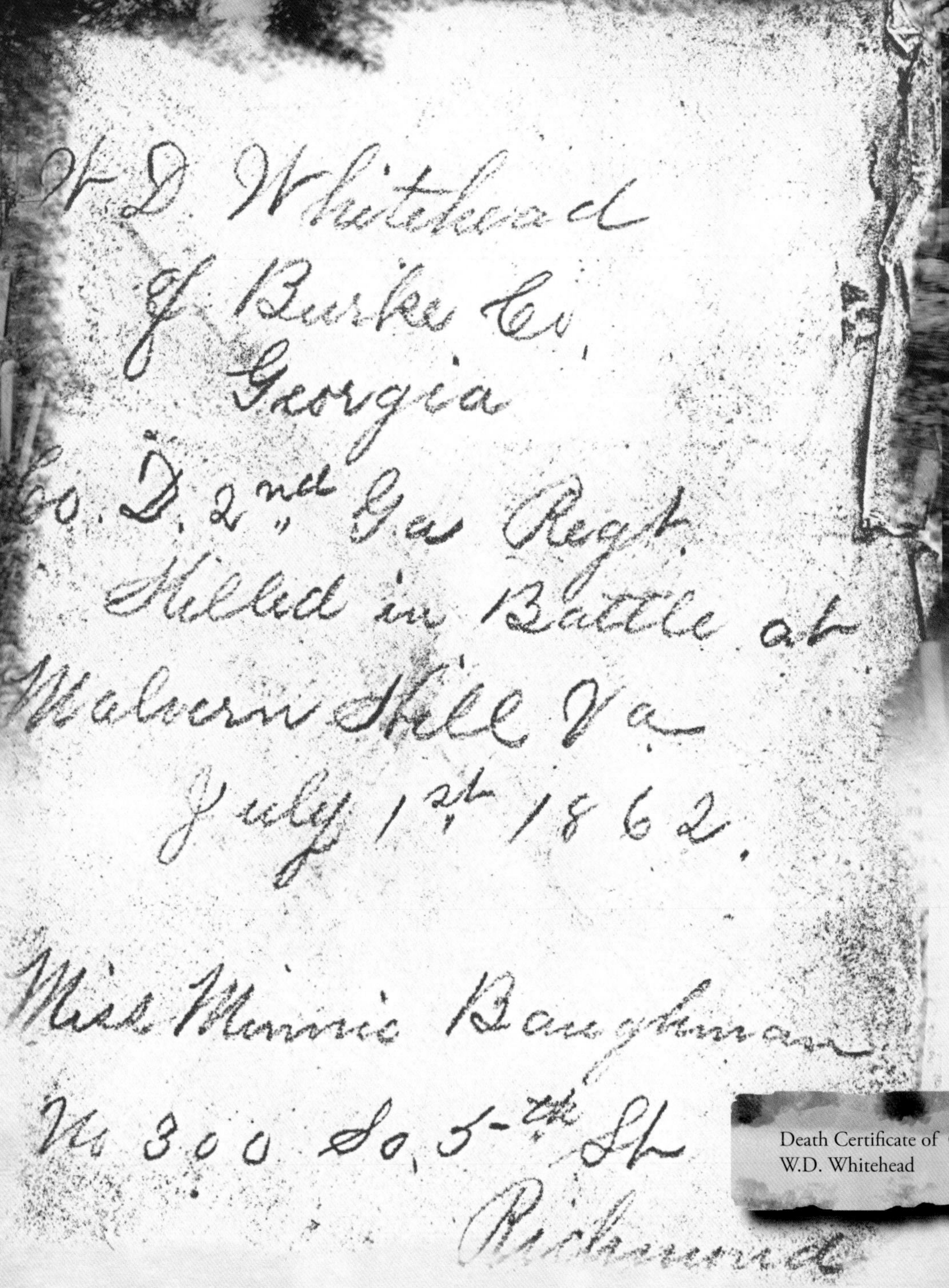

W. D. Whitehead
of Burke Co,
Georgia
Co. D 2nd Ga Regt,
Killed in Battle at
Malvern Hill Va,
July 1st 1862.

Miss Minnie Baughman
No 300 So 5th St
Richmond

Death Certificate of Color Corporal
W.D. Whitehead

Hollywood Confederate Cemetery,
Richmond, Virginia

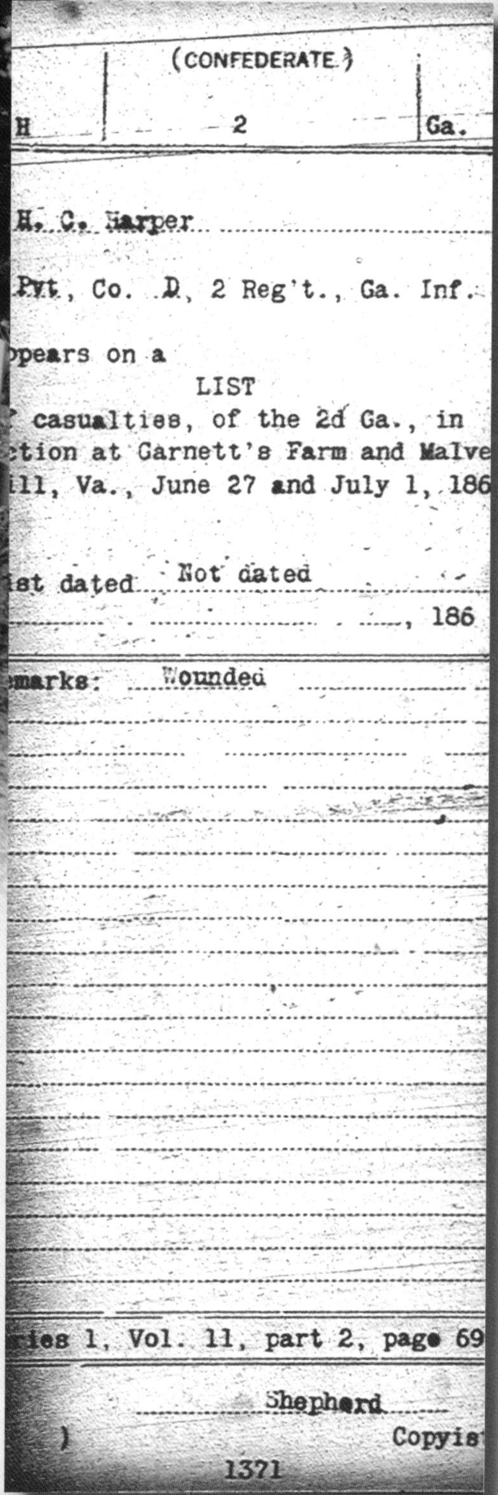

(CONFEDERATE.)

H 2 Ga.

H. C. Harper

Pvt, Co. D, 2 Reg't., Ga. Inf.

ppears on a
LIST
casualties, of the 2d Ga., in
ction at Garnett's Farm and Malve
ll, Va., June 27 and July 1, 186

st dated Not dated
, 186

marks: Wounded

ries 1, Vol. 11, part 2, page 69

Shephard
Copyis

1371

JUNE 29TH - JULY 1ST

(Savages Station, White Oak Swamp, and Malvern Hill) federal casualties were 724 killed, 4,245 wounded, 3,067 missing out of some 83,000 engaged in an army more than 115, 000. Confederate losses were 8,602 killed and wounded and 875 missing, of perhaps 86,500 engaged out of an effective army of 88,000 plus. For whole of the 7 days, the losses were appalling in this still "young" war—confederates over 20,000 casualties including 3,216 killed 16, 000 wounded and 946 missing. Federal casualties totaled nearly 16,000 including 1,734 killed, and 6,053 missing.

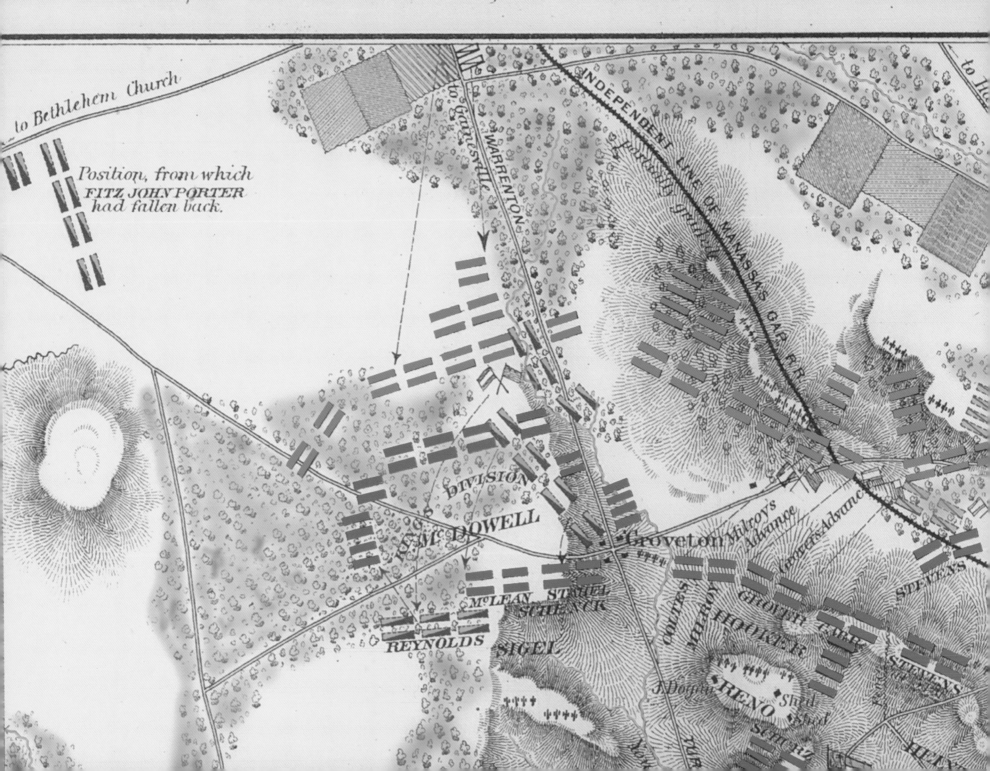

to Bethlehem Church

Position, from which
FITZ JOHN PORTER
had fallen back.

to Gainesville

WARRENTON

INDEPENDENT LINE OF MANASSAS GAP R.R.

to The

DIVISION

McDOWELL

Groveton

Milroys

Krogers Advance

McLEAN SCHENCK SAMUEL

REYNOLDS

SIGEL

KRZY MILROY GROVEN CARR HOOKER

STEVENS

RENO

Shed

J.Dogan

Shed

Sept 17

STEVENS

Manassas
AUGUST 29-30, 1862

After the battle of Malvern Hill, they were marched to Richmond. Then orders were received to go to Northern Virginia to reinforce Stonewall Jackson at Manassas. This march like many others was accompanied by many deprivations, but weary and footsore they reached Thoroughfare Gap, a point for which a race was run between the Yankees and the Second and Sixth Georgia regiments in which the Georgians came out victorious.

Forcing their way through Thoroughfare Gap they arrived at Manassas two days before the battle began on August 29th, lasting through the 30th, and resulting in victory for the Confederates in this fight. Packard and James A. Wray were killed; H. Rawls lost a leg; J. W. Hughes, Tom Miller and W. H. Tompkins were wounded.

After the battle they crossed the Potomac and entered Maryland, the first halt being at Frederick City. While here an election was held to fill the vacancy caused by the death of Lt. Packard, which resulted in the promotion of G. W. Hurst.

Antietam
SEPTEMBER 17, 1862

FROM HERE THE 2ND GA. REGIMENT PROCEEDED TO HAGERSTOWN. After resting here a few days they marched on to Sharpsburg.

On their arrival here then were ordered immediately to take their position in line of battle on the extreme right with the 20th Ga. Regiment to hold Stone Bridge, known to the Federals as Burnside Bridge. At an early hour in the morning of September 17th the battle was opened by the Federals, the corps of Hooker and Mansfield advancing to the attack.

A fierce conflict ensued, in which Co. D., the old Burke Sharpshooters, distinguished themselves for their bravery. For nine weary hours they fought like demons until their ammunition gave out. Several attempts were made to replenish the supply. Col. Wm. R. Holmes sent out to get it himself, but as he started he was shot by the enemy and instantly killed. Lt. H. H. Perry, J. G. Burton and W. R. Cox of Co. D. and Lt. Lewis of Co. B. made every effort to take the body from the battlefield, but the brave group was fired at, and Lt. Lewis and J. G. Burton were wounded, rendering it impossible to move it. So all that was mortal of their comrade was left in the hands of the enemy.*

Having no ammunition, the Second Georgia Regiment was ordered to the rear. The command was obeyed, but in falling in line again it was discovered that Co. D. was missing. Owing to the deafening roar of the cannonry and being in the extreme right, the order was not heard. Lt. Perry was sent back to bring the company and in the rush to reach the regiment, with the firing rapid and continuous, Lt. Hurst was wounded.

Those wounded in this encounter were Lt. G. W. Hurst, J. G. Burton and W. M. Quinney.

*Colnel Holmes was later buried on the battlefield.

No. 388.

C. S. A.

On the morning of September 17, 1862, this bridge was defended by the 2d and 20th Georgia of Toombs' Brigade and the 50th Georgia of Drayton's Brigade. The 20th Georgia was on the high wooded bluff immediately opposite this end of the bridge, and the 2d and 50th Georgia in open order, supported by one company of Jenkins' S.C. Brigade, continued the line to Snavely's Ford. One company of the 20th Georgia was on the narrow wooded strip north of this point between the creek and the Sharpsburg road. Richardson's Battery of the Washington Artillery was posted on the high ground about 500 yards northwest and Eubank's (Va.) Battery on the bluff north of and overlooking the bridge. The artillery on Cemetery Hill commanded the bridge and the road to Sharpsburg.

At 9 A.M. Crook's Brigade of the Ninth Corps, moving from the ridge northeast of the bridge, attempted to cross it but failed. Soon after, the 2d Maryland and 6th New Hampshire, of Nagle's Brigade, charging by the road from the south were repulsed. At 1 P.M. the bridge was carried by an assault of Ferrero's Brigade, and the defenders, after a vain effort to check Rodman's Division, moving by Snavely's Ford on their right flank, fell back to the Antietam Furnace road and reformed on the outskirts of the town of Sharpsburg.

Historical Marker
Antietam Park Service

Above Rohrback Bridge

THE TIME OF THE SCENE IS AROUND 1 P.M., JUST AFTER LIEUTENANT HUDSON DELIVERED THE ORDER TO COLONEL JOHN F. HARTRANFT, OF THE 31ST PA, AND COLONEL ROBERT B. POTTER, OF THE 31ST NY, TO TAKE THE BRIDGE. HUDSON CAN BE SEEN RUNNING BACK UP TO THE KNOLLS.

The 2nd GA is in the foreground with Lieutenant Colonel William R. Holmes in a rifle pit, the remains of which can still be seen on the slope above Rohrbach Bridge. Note that Holmes is carrying a Georgia-made sword and is wearing shoulder knots. Most of the soldiers are wearing Georgia pattern shell jackets and frock coats, many of which had black collars. Note that two soldiers have jackets with the distinctive Georgian 3-point black cuff. The troops carry a variety of long arms, including the 1853 Enfield rifle, the 1842 Musket, and the 1841 "Mississippi" Rifle. The Georgians mostly carried muskets, but the Burke County Sharpshooters, who were present at the west end of the bridge, carried Enfields.

The 20th GA is in the left center on the slope and near the bridge entrance with Lieutenant Farquhard McCrimmon. At this point in the battle, part of the 20th GA was in the process of pulling out, as can be seen by the two figures on the road in the shade. Also note the two soldiers under the bridge arch; they were captured at the end of the battle.

The 51st PA is on the bridge with Captain Allebaugh and the color guard, and to the left behind the stone wall. Colonel Hartranft is at the bridge entrance waving his hat to urge his men forward. The Pennsylvanians carry their distinctive national colors, which were made by Evans & Hassall and have the Pennsylvania state seal in the canton.

The 51st NY is towards the right on the road and milling near the bridge entrance. Colonel Potter is in the road waving his sword; elements of the 48th PA have emerged from the trees on the knolls far center; remnants of the 2nd MD and 6th NH are milling far right; far left are Union batteries and elements of the 28th OH.

Walter G. Buble © 2001
Permission for use.

Fredericksburg

Ford

Peyton

Marye

Howes

Hazel Run

Ferryhough

LONGSTREET'S

CORPS

TELEGRAPH ROAD

Cot

Goodwyn

Deep Run

ENEMY'S LINES

Lt. Gl. LONGSTREET'S
Hd. Qrs.

Owens

GARDINER

CARPENTER'S BAT.

HOOD

DAVIDSONS ½ BAT.
BERNARD BAT.

PENDER

Cabins

LINE

LANE

Gate

RAPPAHA

Fredericksburg
DECEMBER 13, 1862

AFTER THE BATTLE THEY CROSSED THE POTOMAC TO MARTINSBURG, AND HERE SMALLPOX MADE ITS APPEARANCE IN THE 2ND GA. REGIMENT AND NECESSITATED THEIR QUARANTINE FOR TEN DAYS.

When the news came that Burnside had started for Richmond by way of Fredericksburg the 2nd. Ga. Regiment was sent there. The battle of Fredericksburg occurred December 13, 1862. After the battle they went into winter quarters.

When the spring campaign opened they were ordered to Petersburg, from thence to Powhalton. From Powhalton they were ordered to North Carolina. However, before going, two weeks were spent at Dutch Gap canal, between Richmond and Petersburg, and from here they were marched to North Carolina, where they were engaged in foraging for two weeks.

At Petersburg, Lt. Perry was promoted to the rank of Captain and placed with Gen. Benning as Adjutant and Inspector General of that brigade.

Two magnificent armies faced one another here in the middle of December, 1862. Along the ground on the east side of the Rappahannock – the famous Stafford Heights –the men in blue were massed in a long line of camps. In the town were scattered forces of Confederate troops, and along the riverfront each house was a temporary citadel; even cannon frowned from the windows. The winding river, now unbridged and at high water, separated the Army of Northern Virginia under Lee from the Army of the Potomac under Burnside. Fredericksburg, deserted by women, children, the aged, and the infirm, lay helpless before the Federal guns. But along the hill against the horizon stretched Lee's army, under able generals, in an impossible position. Between it and the town lay open ground with a few scattered houses. Stretching across the river were the ruins of the bridges. For a month Burnside had waited for pontoons to enable him to cross in force. On a foggy morning after their arrival, the 11th of December, a landing was effected. The fierce fire of 147 guns from Stafford Heights played havoc among the houses. The sharpshooters that had bothered the pontoniers were driven back, and soon all the Confederate forces had gathered along the ridge a mile to the west of the town. By the 12th, the Federal army had crossed and deployed for battle.

Fredericksburg
A photograph taken just after the Battle of
Fredericksburg, December 1862

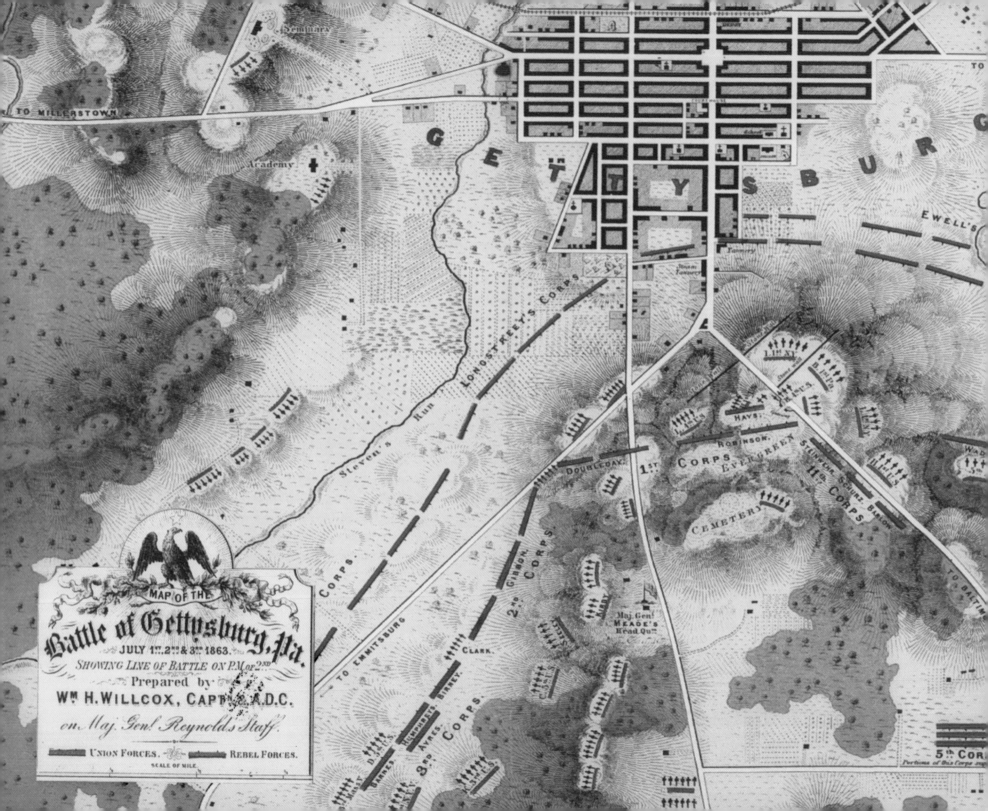

MAP OF THE
Battle of Gettysburg, Pa.
JULY 1ST, 2ND & 3RD 1863.
SHOWING LINE OF BATTLE ON P.M. OF 2ND
Prepared by
Wm. H. Willcox, Capt. & A.D.C.
on Maj. Genl. Reynolds' Staff.

UNION FORCES. ————— REBEL FORCES.
SCALE OF MILE.

GETTYSBURG

TO MILLERSTOWN
Seminary
Academy
Steven's Run
LONGSTREET'S CORPS
EWELL'S
1ST N.Y.
B 1st Pa.
HAYS
KRAUS
ROBINSON
STEINWEHR, SCHURZ, BARLOW
11TH CORPS
WAD
DOUBLEDAY
1ST CORPS
EVERGREEN
CEMETERY
Maj. Genl. MEADE'S Head Qrs.
TO BALTIMORE
CORPS
TO EMMITSBURG
GIBBON
2ND CORPS
KIRBY
CLARK
3RD CORPS
BARNES, HUMPHREYS, BIRNEY, AYRES
D 4TH U.S.
5TH CORPS
Portions of this Corps

Gettysburg
JULY 2, 1863

AT THIS TIME, THE LATTER PART OF APRIL 1863, ORDERS CAME FOR THE 2ND GA REGIMENT TO RETURN TO VIRGINIA. There followed one of the hardest marches of the War. Thirty miles were covered in eight hours in order to reach trains at Petersburg. They joined the Army at Culpepper Courthouse, and here spent a few weeks in recruiting, being recruited and preparing for the campaign in Maryland and Pennsylvania.

At Chambersburg, where they were quartered for eight or ten days, there were new developments. A forced march from Chambersburg to Gettysburg began on the night of July 1st, reaching Gettysburg at sunrise the next morning. Quietness reigned.

Then followed the mortal combat of the Confederacy, of which graphic accounts have been given elsewhere. The wounded in this battle were Lt. Sapp, William R. Cox, James Frost and N. K. Lovett. Hamilton Blount, after being wounded, was taken prisoner and sent to David's Island where he died. A number of others were slightly wounded. Those killed were Lt. G. W. Hurst, Solomon Parker, Raymond Oakman, L. D. Godbee and Alexander Elliott.

Of the many pieces of artillery that were captured by the Confederates in the engagement only three Parrot guns were held and taken from the field, and they were taken by the 2nd Ga. Regiment.

The 2nd Regiment was with the only brigade that broke the enemy's lines on Round Top. Their flag was pierced with eighty minnie balls, evidence of the horrendous battle they had endured.

After the battle they fell back, fording the Potomac River. They recruited near Richmond for three or four weeks.

O**N 2 JULY 1863, FOUR 10-POUNDER PARROT GUNS OF THE 4TH NEW YORK INDEPENDENT BATTERY UNDER THE COMMAND OF CAPTAIN JAMES E. SMITH OCCUPIED HOUCK'S RIDGE, THE HIGH GROUND ABOVE DEVIL'S DEN. FACING WEST, THE GUNS OVERLOOKED THE TIMBERS' HOMESTEAD, THE VALLEY OF ROSE RUN, AND A TRIANGLE FIELD ENCLOSED BY STONE WALLS.**

Around mid-afternoon, the Confederates across the valley near Emmitsburg Road began firing their artillery in advance of their attack towards Little Round Top and the Union left flank. Smith's battery responded with such fury that the attackers thought they faced at least two batteries.

At about 3:30pm, the Confederates of Maj. Gen. John B. Hood's division advanced to the east under fire from the battery. Brig. General E. M. Law's and Brig. General J.B. Robertson's brigades opened the attack on Round Top and Devil's Den. Robertson's 4th and 5th Texas went east directly towards the base of Round Top, while the 1st Texas and 3rd Arkansas veered slightly northeast towards the triangle field below Smith's guns and Rose's Woods to Smith's right.

The 1st Texas approached directly up through the triangle field and traded fire with Smith's Battery, the 124th New York Infantry, and elements of the 4th Maine Infantry. The 3rd Arkansas went into Rose's Woods to battle the 86th New York and 20th Indiana Infantry. During the furious fighting, Smith was heard to shout, "Give them shell! Give them solid shot. Damn them, give them anything!

As the 1st Texas crossed the field and neared the eastern wall, it was driven back by a charge of the 124th New York. Just as the 1st Texas was being driven down the valley, Brig. Gen. H. L. Benning's Georgia Brigade came up. With support from the 2nd, 15th, 17th, and 20th Georgia, the 1st Texas counterattacked, pushing the 124th up to the high ground near the guns.

Smith managed to wheel away one gun and take all of the artillery implements to the rear. A combination of the 1st Texas and the Georgia regiments captured three of Smith's guns and helped occupy Devil's Den along with the 44th and 48th Alabama Infantry.

Smith's battery and the 124th New York managed to hold off the attacking Confederates long enough for Union lines to be established along Little Round Top. While much attention is paid to Joshua Chamberlain and the 20th Maine's defense of Little Round Top, there's little doubt that had the Union defenders of Houck's ridge been less steadfast, the Confederates would have been atop Little Round Top before the Union was prepared to meet them.

Little Round Top
- The Key To Gettysburg -

A "SLAUGHTER PEN" AT GETTYSBURG. On this rocky slope of Little Round Top, Longstreet's men fought with the Federals in the second day's conflict, July 2, 1863. From boulder to boulder they wormed their way, to find behind each a soldier waiting for the hand-to-hand struggle which meant the death of one or the other. After the battle every rock and tree cast a shadow over a victim. The whole tangled and terrible field presented a far more appalling appearance than does the picture, which was taken after the wounded were removed. Little Round Top had been left unprotected by the advance of General Sickles' Third Corps. This break in the Federal line was discovered by General Warren just in time. Hastily procuring a flag, with but two or three other officers to help him he planted it on the hill, which led the Confederates to believe the position was strongly occupied and delayed Longstreet's advance long enough for troops to be rushed forward to meet it. The picture tells all too plainly at what sacrifice the height was finally held.

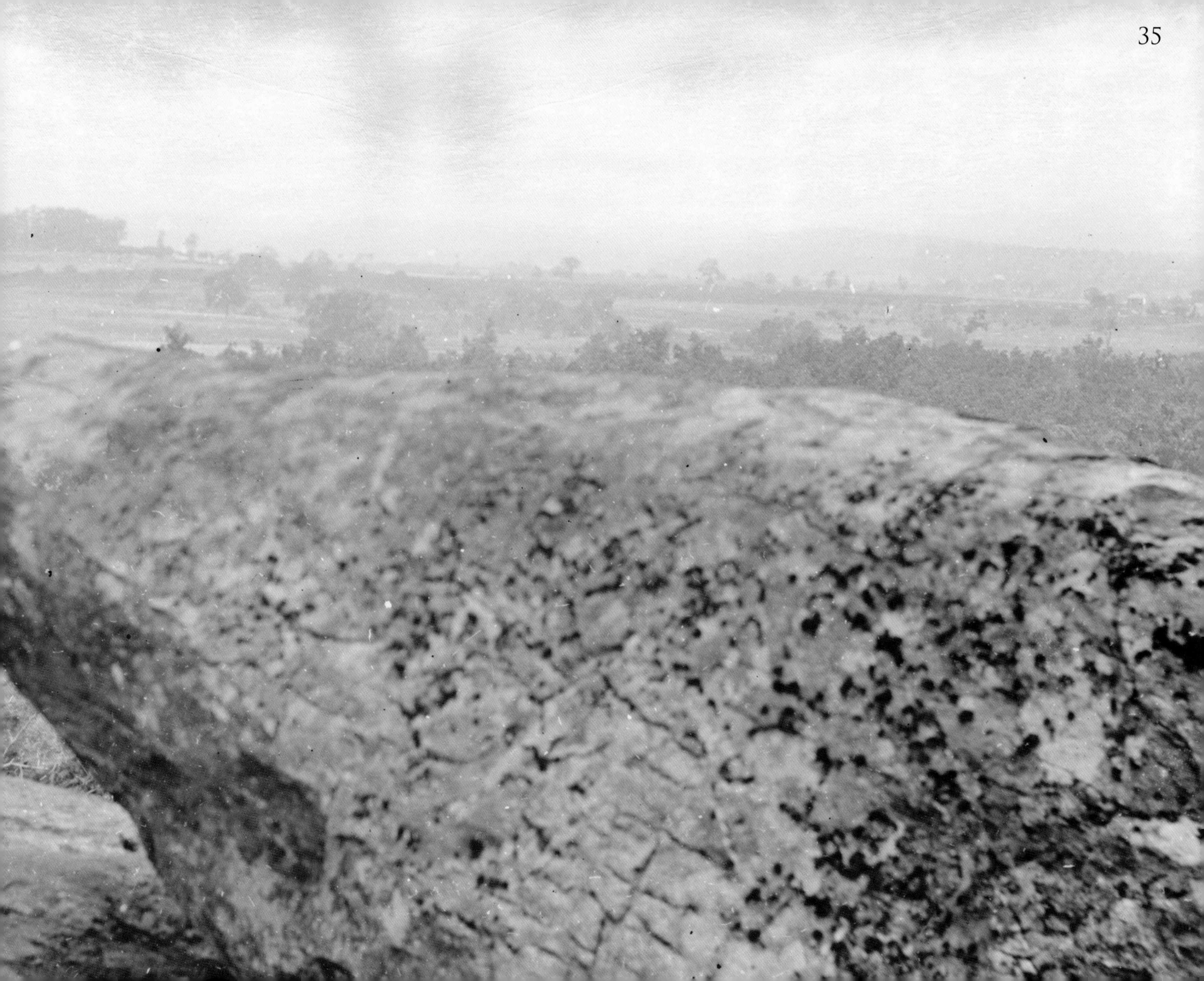

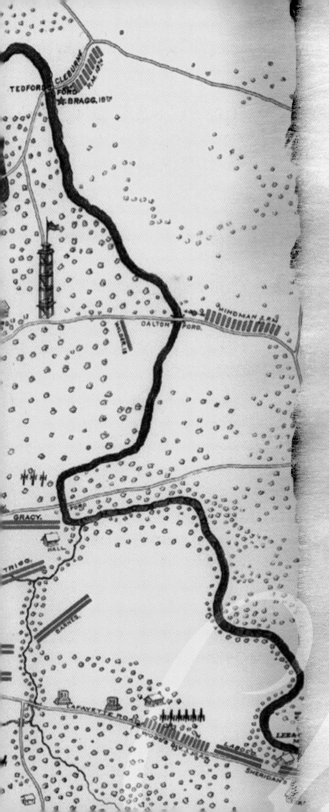

Chickamauga
SEPTEMBER 18-20, 1863

Longstreet's Corps was then ordered to Georgia to reinforce Gen. Bragg at Chickamauga. They arrived there on September 18, 1863, the day before the battle. Gen. Bragg made an attack on Gen. Thomas who was in command of the left of Gen. Rosecram's Army. The battle was hotly contested and battery after battery was taken and retaken. The day closed with no decisive advantage to either side. In this fight a man by the name of McMillen was killed. Capt. W. H. Dickinson was shot through the body with a ram rod, the ball passing through his hat. The Federal soldier who shot him was only ten paces from William H. Blount, who was beside Capt. Dickinson at the time. Blount immediately shot the Yankee and mortally wounded him. He fell at Capt. Dickinson's feet, and Dickinson in a final Supreme act of mercy, ministered to him in his dying moment by giving him water to drink from his own canteen. Bailey Carpenter was shot through the body with a grape shot and died a few days later. W.R. Cox was seriously wounded by a stray ball before the battle began. That night was spent upon the battlefield and the fight was resumed the next morning.

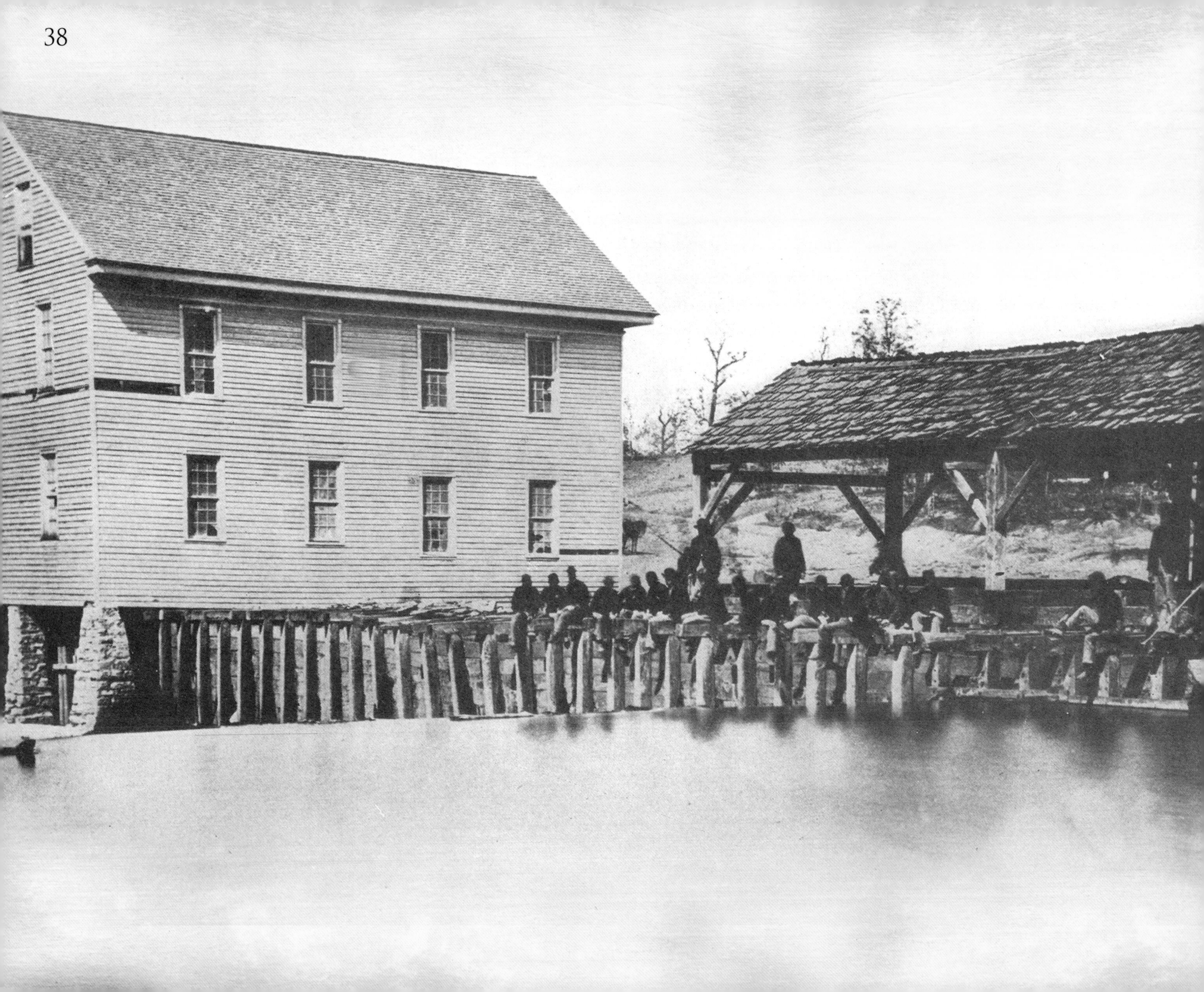

BY THE DENT OF HAND FIGHTING AND THE PROMPT ACTION OF GEN. LONGSTREET, WHO LED HIS MEN INTO A GAP IN THE FEDERAL LINES, THE VICTORY WAS WON BY THE CONFEDERATES. IN THE SECOND DAY'S FIGHT, W. A. BLOUNT WAS WOUNDED, AND F. C. BOSTICK WAS WOUNDED AND DIED THE NEXT DAY. Thomas. E. Blount, color sergeant, was wounded and died. He was wrapped in his blanket and buried in a horse lot at Ringgold, Ga. His grave was dug by Jim Brown, his faithful colored servant of the company. After he was wounded he called to his Colonel saying, "For God's sake Colonel, send some one to take colors, or this will bite the dust." Charlie Jones rushed forward and took the flag.

Lt. B. H. Rogers, who had been assigned to command Company "A," P. C. Wallace and W. D. Tompkins were seriously wounded. George D. Roberts was shot through the foot, after the battery had been captured. Ben Lyrack and B. G. Dye were also wounded. In this battle the 8th Indiana battery was captured and eight beautiful Napolean guns were taken by Benning's brigade. That winter was spent below Richmond on Darbytown Road.

After the battle, companies D & H were consolidated and commanded by Capt. Hancock of Company H, the officers of Company D having all been killed or wounded.

Where The Lines Were Swept Back

Lee & Gordon's mill, seen in the picture, marked the extreme right of the Federal line on the second day at Chickamauga. From it, northward, were posted the commands of McCook and Crittendon, depleted by the detachments of troops the day before to strengthen the left. All might have gone well if the main attack of the Confederates had continued to the left, as Rosecrans expected. But hidden in the woods, almost within a stone's throw of the Federal right on that misty morning, was the entire corps of Longstreet, drawn up in columns of brigades at half distance – "a masterpiece of tactics,: giving space for each column to swing right or left. Seizing a momentous opportunity which would have lasted but thirty minutes at the most, Longstreet hurled them through a gap which, owing to a misunderstanding, had been left open, and the entire Federal right was swept from the field.

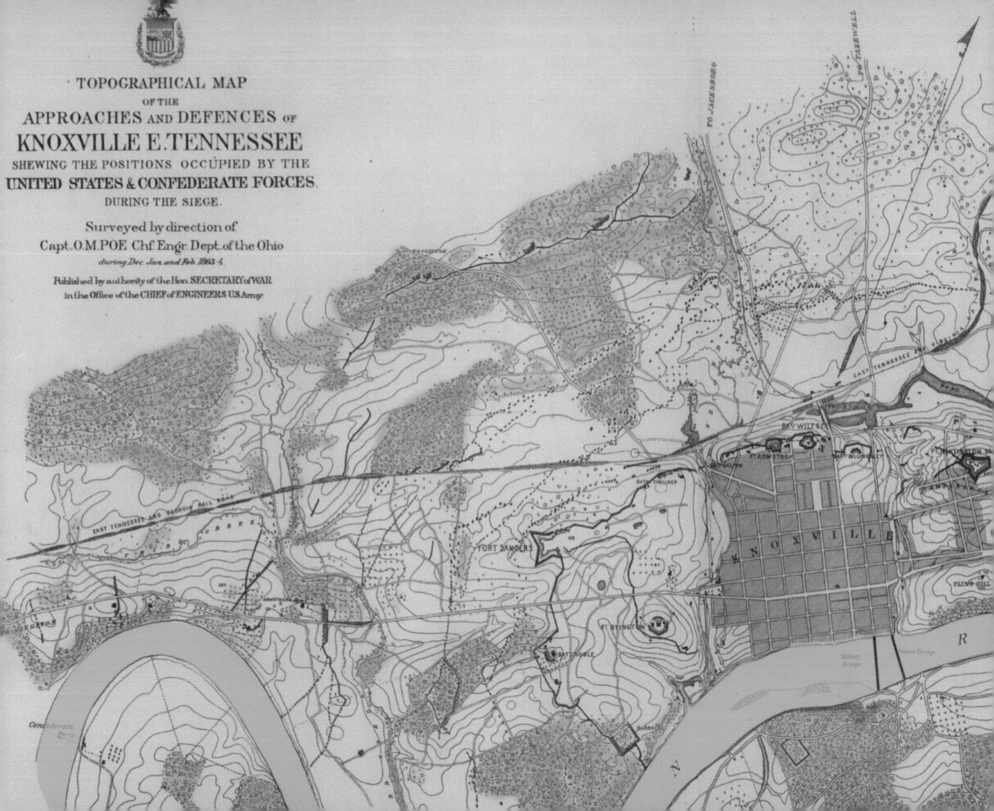

TOPOGRAPHICAL MAP
OF THE
APPROACHES AND DEFENCES OF
KNOXVILLE E. TENNESSEE
SHEWING THE POSITIONS OCCUPIED BY THE
UNITED STATES & CONFEDERATE FORCES.
DURING THE SIEGE.

Surveyed by direction of
Capt. O.M. POE Chf. Engr. Dept. of the Ohio
during Dec. Jan. and Feb. 1863-4.

Published by authority of the Hon. SECRETARY of WAR
in the Office of the CHIEF of ENGINEERS U.S. Army.

Seige of Knoxville
WINTER OF 1863

AFTER THE BATTLE OF CHICKAMAUGA, LONGSTREET'S CORPS WAS DETACHED FROM BRAGG'S ARMY AND SENT TO TENNESSEE TO BESIEGE KNOXVILLE, THAT CITY BEING OCCUPIED BY BURNSIDE AND THE ARMY OF OHIO. He would have held it, for the enemy were on the point of starvation, but for Sherman, who was sent with 25,000 men to reinforce Burnside. This forced Longstreet from East Tennessee where many hardships were encountered.

That winter was spent at Manistown and Strawberry Plain, where all communications were cut off from the outer world. With a scarcity of food and clothing and no shoes, their suffering defied description. While at Strawberry Plain the soldiers found a butcher pen where they obtained raw cowhide for their feet, a poor substitute for shoes.

The Diary Of James E. Harper
February 1864 - April 1865

James E. Harper was
discharged from the Burke
Sharpshooters in March
1862 due to typhoid fever. He
returned to his home in
Augusta, GA and remained
there until February 20, 1864
when he left home to join the
27th Georgia Infantry in
Charleston, SC. At that time
he started a diary which gives an
account of his service as a
Confederate soldier until his unit
surrendered at Greensboro,
NC in April 1865. Entries
from his diary follow:

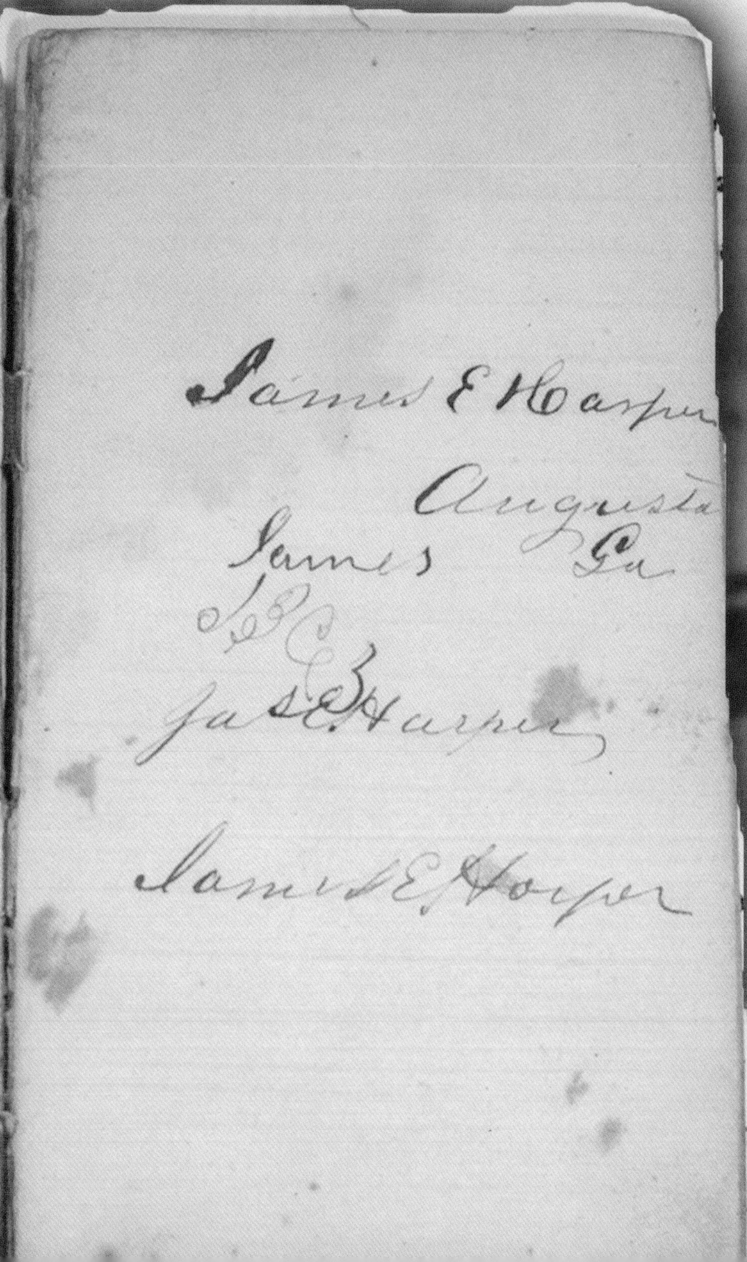

James E Harper
Augusta
James Ga
ASC
Jas E Harper

James E Harper

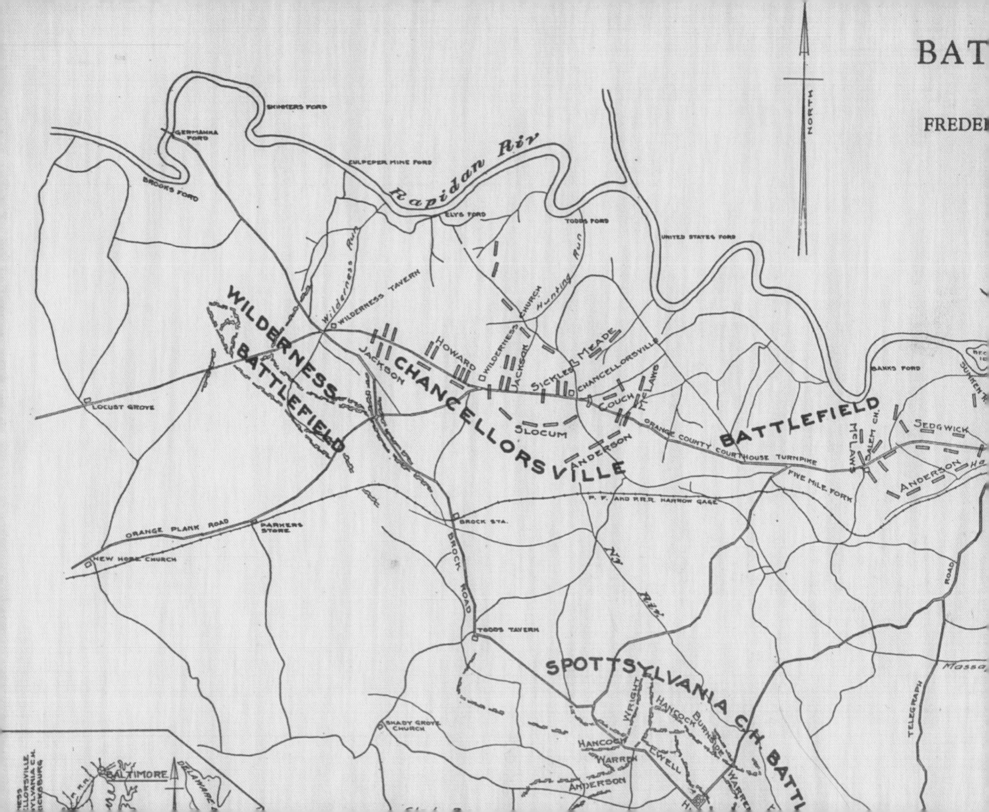

EFIELD MAP

OF THE

BURG ~ SPOTSYLVANIA

TLEFIELD PARK

PUBLISHED BY

RT A. KISHPAUGH

DERICKSBURG, VA.

Wilderness
MAY 5-7, 1864

Spotsylvania
MAY 9, 1864

I N APRIL 1864, THEY WERE ORDERED TO VIRGINIA. They went by rail wherever the roads were not torn up. Reaching Gordonsville a force march was ordered - with all the hardships imaginable attending out to the Wilderness, and here from the 5th to 7th May, one of the hardest contested battles of the War was fought, which resulted in favor of the Confederates. In it, R. A. Hankinson, Floyd Cox, and Robert Boyd were killed, Capt. W. H. Dickinson lost his arm. H. H. Wallace and W. H. Lovett were wounded.

From there they went to Spotsylvania and engaged in another battle on the 9th of May. There were no casualties. Next was an encounter at Hanover Junction.

April 25th 1864

Took Cass at sundown yesterday for Savannah. Reached the City before daylight. Am just now leaving by rail for Charleston, S.C. Rumors of our being ordered to Virginia are current.

April 30th 1864

Upon our arrival at Charleston, S.C., on the afternoon of the 25th inst., we "bivouacked" near the depot for the night. The next day we moved in the direction of James Island, but had not gone far before we were ordered to halt. After remaining a day here, we again moved in the direction of the Island, it was said to hold Dills Bluff. Had nearly reached this point when we were ordered back to Charleston. We all felt sure, now, that we would go to Virginia. In this we were agreeably mistaken, for the next day we were sent to Legon's Point, James Island at which we now are.

May 5th, 1864

The Post of Logon's Point being under command of Col. Zachry, he has detailed me, for the present, as a Clerk in his office, to assist in writing etc.

May 7th, 1864

Rumors of our being ordered to Virginia are again current. Would much prefer to campaign here than there. With an eyeglass, Morris Island and its surroundings are distinctly visible. Even the men who are engaged in loading the guns which so constantly are leveled against Ft. Sumpter can be seen. Battered Gregg now has the hated ensign of the once venerated Union flying from its flagstaff.

May 11th, 1864

We left James Island today for Virginia.

May 20th, 1864

After various delays upon the way, we reached Weldon, N.C. a few days ago, where we are now stationed in apprehension of a raid being made against this point by the enemy.

May 21st, 1864

Reached Petersburg, Va., today and are ordered to the Lines between the James and Appomattox Rivers.

May 24, 1864

The enemy shelled our lines vigorously last night. No one was hurt however.

May 29th, 1864

Having left the South lines this morning, we have just reached Cold Harbor on the North Lines and taken position in front of the enemy.

May 31st, 1864

We have been engaged yesterday and today in throwing up

breastworks under fire of enemy's sharpshooters.

June 2nd, 1864

Regt. engaged yesterday at Cold Harbor— loss about 70 killed and wounded. Enemy repulsed.

June 4th, 1864

Enemy made a general assault against our lines yesterday in some places, advancing for 5 or 6 times after as many repulses. Douglas of Co I killed, 'Enemy at length driven back with great loss.'

June 10th, 1864

Since our arrival here, sharpshooting has been carried on with considerable effect by both sides. One cannot raise his head above the works without the risk of being fired at by the ever watchful sharpshooters.

June 16th, 1864

Reached the lines in front of Petersburg last night. Found the enemy in possession of our breastworks, the militia having been driven out. Formed line of battle during the night a few hundred yards in front, and by hard work have now a line of earthworks confronting those lost by the militia.

June 18th, 1864

Fell back a half of a mile during last night to a more advantageous position from which our artillery could be used to more advantage. Enemy about sunrise today advanced against our works but were easily repulsed, Lt. Col Gardner killed.

June 19th, 1864

During last night the enemy threw up earthworks a few hundred yards in our front. Brisk sharpshootlng is now going on, with serious loss to us. The enemy are also erecting mortar batteries which will annoy us a great deal.

June 24th, 1864

Hagood's Brigade assaulted enemy's lines today, but were repulsed with considerable loss. Our Regt. was held in reserve but was not ordered to the attack.

CHAR[LES]

FIELD OF WA[R]

Halfway House
Kingsland Cr.
Cox's Ferry
Cox
Atkins' Ldg.
Jones Neck
Turkey Cr.
Haxall
Proctor's Cr.
Chesterfield Sta.
Red Water Cr.
Dutch Gap
Trent's Reach
Curl's Nck.
Carters
Mason's Pt. Ldg.
McClellan Herring Cr.
1862 Ldg.
West
Chesterfield CH.
Hornet House Bat.
Bermuda Hundred
Ulster
Eppes
Berkley
West
Walthall Junct.
Butler's Hd.Q.
Lighthouse or Bakehouse Cr.
Pt. of Rocks
Lt. Ho.
Jordan's
Coggins Pt.
Swift Cr.
Port Walthall
Genl. Grant's Hd.Q.
Franks Br.
Cedar Level
Clarke
Garysville
Brandon Br.
Clifton
City Point R.R.
Gd. Pitkins
Old Town
Bailey's Cr.
Powells Cr.
Pocahontas
Birney
Appomattox Riv.
Old CH.
Canal
Side or Lynchburg R.R.
Meade
South Side or Lynchburg R.R.
PETERSBURG
Bradford
Pr. George CH.
Weldon Plank & R.R.
Avery House
Hancock
Col. Avery neck Ldg.
Jones House

PRINCE GEOR[GE]

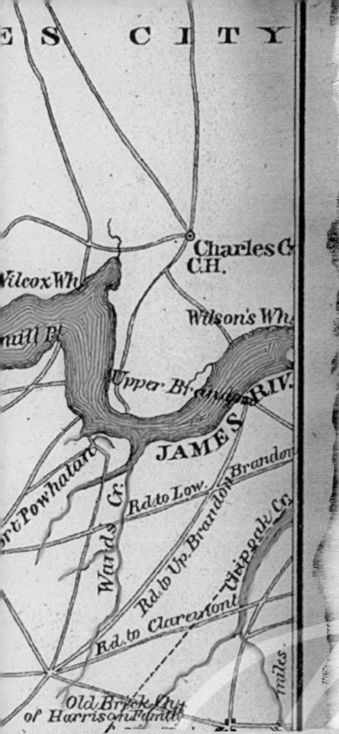

ROUND RICHMOND & PETERSBURG 1864-5.

By Andrew B. Cross — Baltimore.

Petersburg
JULY 1, 1864 - SPRING 1865

THERE FOLLOWED ONE FIGHT AFTER ANOTHER THROUGHOUT THE SUMMER. In a skirmish at Deepbottom, B. F. Lynch was shot and killed by a Federal Sharpshooter.

In front of Petersburg, Thomas Eliott was also killed by a sharpshooter.

52

Entrance to Crater
July 1864

July 1st, 1864

The casualties in the Regt. have been much smaller of late. During first two days on these lines, our Regt. lost 10 killed and about 30 wounded, most of them severely.

July 5th, 1864

Every preparation was made yesterday to receive an attack from the enemy, but contrary to all expectation, the day passed off quietly.

July 10th, 1864

Have been in trenches since the 15th. Without any relief except for 2 days. We are all becoming completely fagged out from want of rest. We get only three hours sleep at night, one half of the men being up from 9 to 12, the other from 12 to 3 O'clock, when all fall in lines and remain with arms and accoutrements on until day light.

July 15th 1864

One month in trenches today. Heat very oppressive, no shade trees being near our position

July 20th, 1864

It having rained all day yesterday, the trenches are now very muddy, rendering locomotion anything but pleasant.

26th July, 1864

Were relieved by Martin's Brigade last. The night and day before it rained continuously. Having no shelter, we were rendered very uncomfortable.

29th July, 1864

Relieved a portion of Field's Div. on the right last night. No picket firing here. Branch running between the opposing pickets used by both parties.

30th July, 1864

At about 5 A.M. this morning was startled by a violent shaking of the earth, followed almost instantaneously by a tremendous explosion. The guns upon both sides then opened and the cannonading exceeded any I have ever heard. Soon the loud "Huzza" of the Yankees was heard as they rushed to the assault of our lines. It soon became known to us that the Federals had "sprung a mine" a short distance to our left and were endeavoring to break through the lines during the confusion thus made. They gained a momentary success, but were driven back with fearful loss by Mason's Div., then in reserve. For the first time negro troops have been pitted against the Army of N. Va. They met, indeed, with a bloody fate, thousands having been slain in this reckless attempt.

July 31st, 1864

Visited scene of the late "Blow-Up" this morning. It almost beggars description. The mangled bodies of the dead and dying were being dug from the mass of superincumbent earth, huge boulders were thrown up between which the bloody remains of some ill fated soldiers had been crushed. In some cases, the clothing had been burned off the bodies. White or black, friend or foe lay mingled together in one mighty mass of putrefaction. The intense heat of the sun caused this to take place sooner than is usual. The enemy's loss in killed, wounded etc. was about 6000, ours 1500. "Man's inhumanity to man has, indeed, made countless thousands mourn."

August 2nd, 1864

We were relieved last night by a portion of Field's Div., and after a march of 4 miles, reached our old Reserve Post, near Iron Bridge.

August 4th, 1864

Indications having been pretty strong for some time that the enemy are again engaged in mining, we have been engaged in mining also.

August 5th, 1864

Notwithstanding that we were Informed of the intention of our authorities to spring a mine at a certain hour today, we were considerably startled when the explosion did take place. It was not Intended to make any assault, but the whole affair was merely experimental. It, of course, caused the usual cannonading and sharpshootlng to be increased. No one hurt on our lines.

Fort Mahone - " Fort Damnation"

August 14th, 1864

Today is the Sabbath. How discordant are the sounds which greet the ear! The mellow peals of the solemn church bell heard in the distance is disenchanted in a great measure of its pleasing associations by the sharp crack of the rifle, the loud whiz of the parrott shell & the heavy boom of the mortars telling in unmistakable terms of the deadly feud existing between man and man. How different too are our enforced duties from those which should engage our time. Oh! That the measure of our chastisement had been filled and we became a God fearing people , that He would grant us peace with the establishment of our National Independence.. And make us that "happy and peculiar people whose God is the Lord." It is now raining hard and as we go to the front tonight I anticipate anything but a pleasant time.

August 21st, 1864

Rained again yesterday. Having discarded shoes and stockings and rolled up my pantaloons, I made my way along the lines, rather a pitiful looking object, I know. What would my Augusta friends have thought to have seen me thus.

August 22nd, 1864

Rained again yesterday. While filling my canteen at well with a comrade, he was shot down, the ball just passing me.

August 28th, 1864

Very heavy mortar firing last night, The emeny also shelled the city furiously.

August 30th, 1864

City and lines again shelled furiously last night. New kind of shell employed by the enemy. It resembles a mortar at first, but upon exploding separates into seven or 8 balls of fire which slowly descend. It is probably designed to fire the City.

September 11th, 1864

Life in trenches is pretty much the same as formerly. The constant vigilance required is very trying to one's powers of endurance.

September 12th, 1864

Repartee after repartee past between the pickets today. To hear them joking with each other it would not seem likely that the same men could in a short while engage in a death struggle with each other.

September 14th, 1864

Appointed Sgt. Major today.

September 26th, 1864

Were ordered to front lines last night. This morning are ordered back to take part in inspection of div. by Gen'l Lee, preparatory it is thought of going to the Valley.

October 2nd, 1864

On the afternoon of the 30th inst. 27th GA. formed a part of the forces which assaulted Ft. Harrison. *The assault was unsuccessful, 27th GA.'s loss was 2 killed and about 20 wounded and missing. The night of the assault it commenced raining and has continued off and on for 3 days. Having no shelter, we of course had a disagreeable time of it. We commenced throwing up a new line of works confronting Harrison last night. Are now well prepared for any aggressive movement which our reverses of the 30th may embolden the enemy to make.

*The 2nd Georgia participated in this assault.

October 3rd, 1864

After our repulses at Ft. Harrison, a wounded man from Clemmons Brigade lay for three nights and two days between the opposing picket lines. The enemy not suffering us to remove him and we not allowing them as the wounded man signified to us his unwillingness to be taken prisoner. He was finally secured at great peril on the third night.

December 11th, 1864

We moved down to the Darby Town Road and our Division having joined Field's we both advanced against the enemy driving in their pickets with small loss. General Longstreet having accomplished his project, namely, a reconnaissance, of the enemy's position, ordered us back to camp at dark. Such a march as we had, I have rarely experienced. The morning's snow having mostly melted during the day caused the roads to be in a wretched condition. I was muddied to my knees. Stopped by and took a cup of coffee with HCH* and reached camp by 9 o'clock having marched during the day about ten miles.

*His brother Henry Clay Harper

Catharine Whitehead Rowland Journal

OCTOBER 1863 – JANUARY 1865

ATHARINE WHITEHEAD ROWLAND (1838-1917) WAS THE DAUGHTER OF AMOS GRATTAN AND ELIZABETH MCKINNE WHITEHEAD, THE OWNER OF IVANHOE PLANTATION NEAR WAYNESBORO, GA. During the War, Catharine's husband, Charles Alden Rowland, was an officer and Catharine remained with her child at Ivanhoe.

On Thursday, October 29th, 1863, she began a journal which she maintained until November 30th, 1878. Portions of her journal follow.

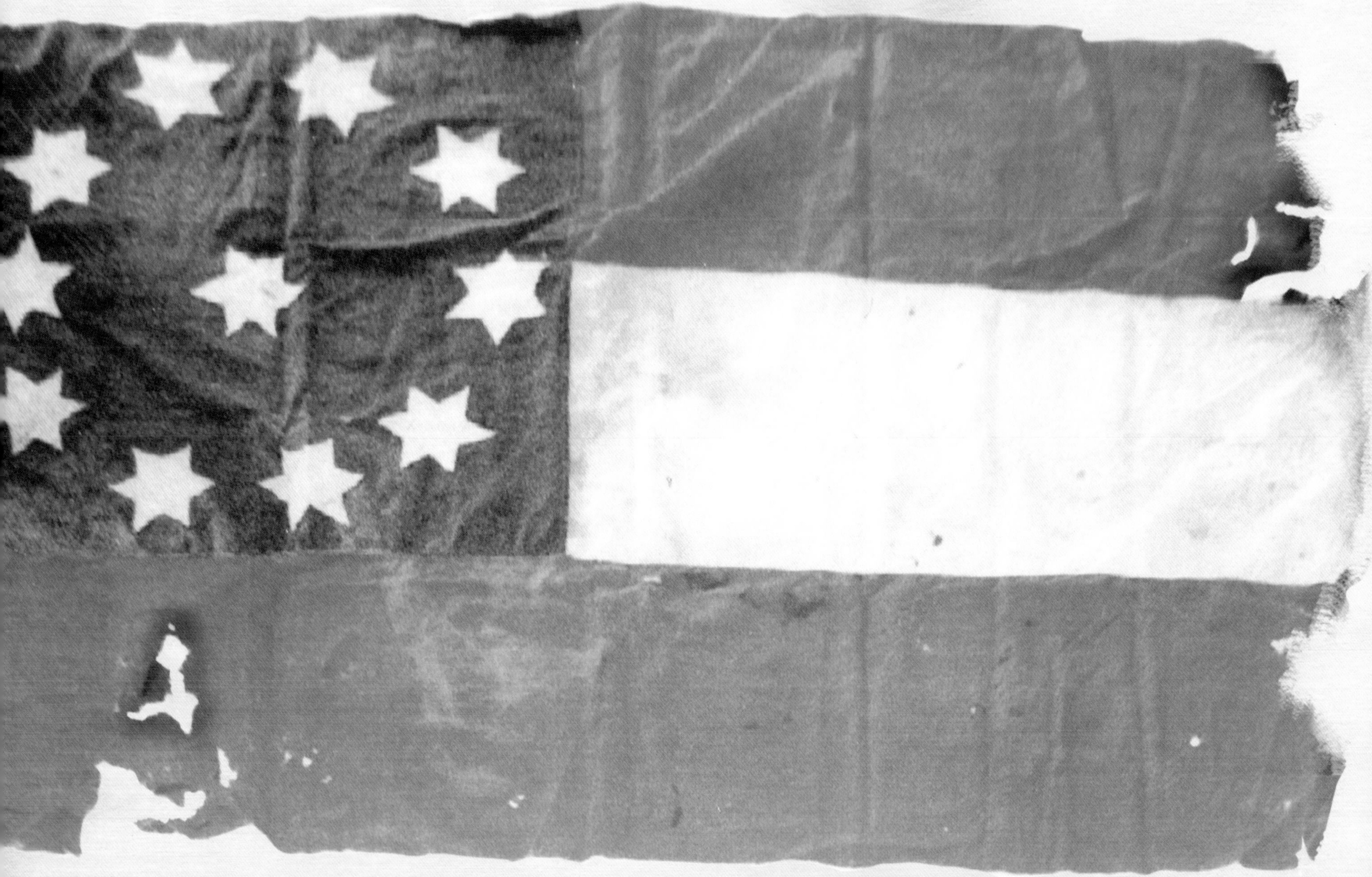

October 29th, 1863

I have been intending since Charlie went away from me to commence a journal, to be kept on during his absence, but I have been prevented from making a beginning until tonight. It has long been a desire of mine to keep a journal yet I cannot tell why I have never done so. I regret not having commenced at the beginning of this war, as so many stirring events have been transpiring around us, I should like to have noted them down. I expect yet, however, my journal shall prove interesting as I do not think this war is likely to end for many years to come. …

Wednesday, November 9, 1864

Today has been as warm as Spring & really oppressive. I was engaged all the morning in teaching Mary & intend to keep her close at her books & not allow anything to interfere. Father went up to Augusta this afternoon & Mother & I went in to Waynesboro to make some visits & carried Mary & Willie with us. I had a pleasant visit both to Aunt Harlow & Mrs. Carter & we also went to see Mrs. Maharry & Mrs. Jones, but they were not at home. I miss Miss Julia very much indeed & when I went to my room last night it looked desolate enough without her. No letter again to-day from Charlie though I hope I shall hear by tomorrow's mail.

Mrs. Rogers sent Mother word that she had the original battle flag of the 2d Regiment if she would like to see it so we stopped by this afternoon just before leaving Waynesboro. It made my heart ache when I looked at what remained of it for it is shot almost to pieces & I thought of my darling, noble *Brother, who was the first to fall in bearing that flag. Oh! would that his life could have been spared, but God who doeth all things well knew what was best for us & I know it was all right that my precious Will should have been called away & it is cruel to wish him back when he is enjoying such bliss in the presence of the Saviour he loved & served so well. I wish we could have the flag as I am sure we would prize it more than any one else, but it has been sent by the company to be placed in the court-house at Waynesboro. Mrs. Rogers allowed Mother to bring it home for a few days as she wanted Father & the servants to see it. The servants were all very much affected when they looked upon it, particularly Mammy who wept very much.

*W.D. Whitehead See Page 16

Headquarters Military Division Of The Mississippi
In The Field
Kingston, Georgia
November 9, 1864

1. For the purpose of military operations, this army is divided into two wings, viz.:

2. The right wing, Major-General O. O. Howard, commanding, composed of the Fifteenth and Seventeenth Corps; the left wing, major-General H. W. Slocum commanding, composed of the Fourteenth and Twentieth Corps.

3. The habitual order of march will be, wherever practicable, by four roads, as nearly parallel as possible, and converging at points hereafter to be indicated in orders. The cavalry, Brigadier-General Kilpatrick commanding, will receive special orders from the commander-in-chief.

4. There will be no general train of supplies, but each corps will have its ammunition-train and provision-train, distributed habitually as follows: Behind each regiment should follow one wagon and one ambulance; behind each brigade should follow a due proportion of ammunition-wagons, provision-wagons, and ambulances. In case of danger, each corps commander should change this order of march, by having his advance and rear brigades unencumbered by wheels. The separate columns will start habitually at 7 a.m., and make about fifteen miles per day, unless otherwise fixed in orders.

5. The army will forage liberally on the country during the march. To this end, each brigade commander will organize a good and sufficient foraging party, under the command of one or more discreet officers, who will gather, near the route traveled, corn or forage of any kind, meat of any kind, vegetables, corn-meal, or whatever is needed by the command, aiming at all times to keep in the wagons at least ten days' provisions for his command, and three days' forage. Soldiers must not enter the dwellings of the inhabitants, or commit any trespass; but, during a halt or camp, they may be permitted to gather turnips, potatoes, and other vegetables, and to drive in stock in sight of their camp. To regular foraging-parties must be intrusted the gathering of provisions and forage, at any distance from the road traveled.

6. To corps commanders alone is intrusted the power to destroy mills, houses, cotton-gins, etc.; and for them this general principle is laid down: In districts and neighborhoods where the army is unmolested, no destruction of such property should be permitted; but should guerrillas or bushwhackers molest our march, or should the inhabitants bomb bridges, obstruct roads, or otherwise manifest local hostility, then army commanders should order and enforce a devastation more or less relentless, according to the measure of such hostility.

7. As for horses, mules, wagons, etc., belonging to the inhabitants, the cavalry and artillery may appropriate freely and without limit; discriminating, however, between the rich, who are usually hostile, and the poor and industrious, usually neutral or friendly. Foraging-parties may also take mules or horses, to replace the jaded animals of their trains, or to serve as pack-mules for the regiments of brigades, in all foraging, of what-ever kind, the parties engaged will refrain abusive or threatening language, and may, where the officer in command thinks proper, give written certificates of the facts, but no receipts; and they will endeavor to leave with each family a reasonable portion for their maintenance.

8. Negroes who are able-bodied and can be of service to the several columns may be taken along; but each army commander will bear in mind that the question of supplies is a very important one, and that his first duty is to see to those who bear arms.

9. The organization, at once, of a good pioneer battalion for each army corps, composed if possible of Negroes, should be attended to. This battalion should follow the advance-guard, repair roads and double them if possible, so that the columns will not be delayed after reaching bad places. Also, army commanders should practise the habit of giving the artillery and wagons the road, marching their troops on one side, and instruct their troops to assist wagons at steep hills or bad crossings of streams.

10. Captain O. M. Poe, chief-engineer, will assign to each wing of the army a pontoon-train, fully equipped and organized; and the commanders thereof will see to their being properly protected at all times.

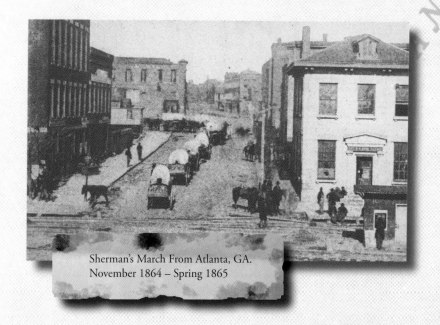

Sherman's March From Atlanta, GA.
November 1864 – Spring 1865

Tuesday, November 29th, 1864

Three days have passed since I opened my journal and I have been through fiery trials since then, having had a visit from the Yankees, but God was most merciful unto us and though we have met with heavy losses, he has given us many blessings & much to be thankful for. We sat up all Saturday night feeling afraid to lie down not knowing at what time the Yankees might come upon us. About three O'clock that morning Mr Sturges came out from Waynesboro saying they entered that place about twelve O'clock, a detachment of 600 having been sent down to destroy the railroad, he remained here until daylight & then went on to Greens Cut to keep the train from going any farther, the bridge having been burnt over Brier Creek. We had breakfast very early & then waited in painful anxiety the arrival of our dreadful foe. They came out about ten O'clock & it is a day long to be remembered.

Mother & I went out & met them as politely as possible knowing it would be best for us. This detachment was under command of Capt Estes, Kilpatrick's adjutant-general & they waited here until four O'clock in the afternoon when Kilpatrick came up with the main body of his army, about 10,000 strong. They all dismounted & Kilpatrick established himself here for the night, bringing in his flag & making this his headquarters. They had not been here however more than half an hour when they commenced moving off very rapidly much to my delight, but I little dreamed the cause, little thought deliverance was so near at hand. The entire command had not moved off when the shouts of Wheeler's men were heard & they commenced firing upon the Yankees just in front of our house they had quite a sharp skirmish just at the top of the hill though there was no one killed. A great

number of balls fell in the yard & in the grove in front of the house & one passed through the kitchen. The first detachment of Yankees behaved very well considering they were Yankees, but they were all most audacious in their manners & walked about as if everything belonged to them: they only stole all the mules & horses & all meat from the smoke house, but when Kilpatrick came up with the main body of his army they, commenced the work of destruction, & they committed every kind of depredation. They broke open the store room & stole every thing, left nothing, poured the syrup all over the floor & sprinkled the flour & sugar all over the yard what they could not carry off, filled the lard with trash & did every thing that was mean & vile. They killed up the turkeys & chickens which they did by throwing the cut glass tumblers & china at them & cutting off their heads. They are certainly the vilest wretches that ever lived & must be overtaken in their wickedness, but if they are not punished in this world, God will certainly punish them in the world to come. They took all the harness about the place & cut it into strings & stole every thing in the shape of tin & wooden ware. They did not confine themselves to stealing from us but took every thing from the negroes, at which I was much sur'prised as they profess to love them so much, they stole all their clothes & money & whatever would be at all useful to themselves, leaving nothing in the shape of tin & but very few cooking utensils. They seem to be fighting for plunder for they asked all the negroes where the silver was & they told them it had been sent to Augusta & no doubt they were much disappointed in not finding it. They made no search for any valuables & found nothing we had buried. Even Kilpatrick asked for the silver, & when the General condescends to anything of the kind you cannot expect anything more from the men. There was a Soldier here from Michigan named Whitehead & when he saw our dipper with the silver plate upon it bearing Father's name, he took it & marched off with it saying it belonged to him, & then had the audacity to ask if we were related, I felt like taking off his head. They all asked for Father & it was a most fortunate circumstance that he was in Augusta or he would doubtless have been taken prisoner, they had a good many citizens with them the day they were here but I understand they have since released them all.

Our house was kept from being pillaged for which we cannot feel too thankful. Capt Estes, at Mothers request, placed a guard around the house as soon as he came out & kept his men from plundering; the guard was kept up until the command commenced moving off when it was withdrawn & then two thieves entered the house for the purpose of stealing, commenced cursing Mother & I in the most outrageous manner asking for money & other valuables & searching all through the lower part of the house, breaking open Mothers desk to look for money. Just then the shouts of Wheelers men were heard & they jumped on their horses & skedaddled in a hurry & thus we were saved from having our house rifled. The Yankees burnt the gin house with twenty-five bales of cotton, the stables & all fodder & set fire to the corn crib but Wheeler came up before it had burnt very far & the servants put it out. The Yankees used up an entire crib of corn in feeding their horses, but we have half a crib left & some corn yet ungathered in the fields, & all our hogs & cattle are left to us so we will not starve. God has certainly been most merciful to us & we should render unceasing praises to Him for all His goodness, my heart is overflowing with gratitude & thankfulness for all His kindness unto us.

All of our negroes remained faithful & though they were offered every inducement to go off with the Yankees not one of them left, except Alfred who was with the horses in the swamp & when they found the horses they made him go along to carry them. Grandison, Jacob & Frank have immortalized themselves & stood

by us more like brothers than servants & I feel we can never do too much for them. An officer said he wished dinner prepared for six officers, & it was very galling to me to see them sitting at our table where we had so often sat & I could scarcely refrain from expressing my feelings but I felt it was best for me to say nothing. It was very hard for me to keep silent but I hope I shall one day meet them on neutral ground where I can give expression to my feelings.

Our men were passing nearly all Sunday night, & Monday morning commenced fighting the Yankees just below Waynesboro & fought them all day, we could hear the cannonading, but it did not sound in the direction of the Savannah road which route we hoped the Yankees had taken; but as if they were going back to Louisville where they had left Sherman with his infantry. Bud John came out Monday night from Waynesboro having heard of our losses, & he felt so anxious to hear the extent of them that he went to Waynesboro from Greens Cut (where he had been since Sunday morning), & then walked out from Waynesboro, he left us this morning for Augusta & I hope he will be able to reach there & let Father know something of us as I know he is anxious about us. We have heard nothing definite from the enemy to-day & have heard no firing so I hope they are some distance from us. Mr Scales came over from his place this afternoon to express his sympathy for us in our trouble & a more warm hearted man I never saw, he is certainly a noble man with a big heart, he told us the Yankees had not visited him at all & insisted upon our sending over to his place & getting some meat & anything else we wanted which was certainly very generous. Cousin Gid was with him & said the Yankees burnt nothing for him, but stole all Cousin Sarah & Rosa's clothing & carried off what silver they could find. The Yankees visited Cousin

Randolph but burnt nothing for him, stole all his horses & mules & killed his cows, they entered his house however & stole all his clothing & bedding & no one being at home, set fire to the house, but the negroes put it out after they left. Mr Morris was entirely burnt out & lost a great deal of cotton & his own negroes set fire to his dwelling & burnt it down which is truly dreadful I think but the Yankees told them they would be back the next day & if the house was still standing would kill them & I suppose they were afraid not to burn it. Bud John says the Yankees burnt the Depot at Waynesboro, the post office & Mr Atterways shop, & Mr James Atterways house as they thought he owned the shop. Wheeler pressed them so close they burnt nothing more, but there is no telling what they might have done had he not come upon them. I feel it is a great deal better for us to have remained as I am sure we saved our house by it, though it was a great trial, & I endured a great mental anxiety & suffering. If Cousin Susan had remained at home she would have saved her house, but she was so frightened when she heard they were coming she went in to Waynesboro. Our Soldiers say the Yankees burn all unoccupied dwellings. I expect Charlie is feeling very anxious about us now as they have doubtless heard by this time of Sherman having left Atlanta for Augusta or Savannah; he told me before he left home that if I should ever hear of the Yankees coming I must go to Augusta, but I could not feel it my duty to leave Mother alone & I am delighted that I remained. Dolly had a son, born the day the Yankees were here & I named it Wheeler after Gen— Wheeler as he was an instrument in God's hand in delivering us from the Yankees.

Wednesday, November 30th, 1864

We went to bed last night for the first time since the Yankees came & were called up at 1 O'clock by Jacob who told us he thought the Yankees were crossing the old field, going from the Louisville into the Augusta road, as he heard the voices of persons talking & the noise of wagons. Mother & I got up at once & dressed, thinking in all probability it might be Sherman with the infantry as the Yankees told us the other day they would come this road. At daylight however we were very much relieved to hear that they were our Soldiers, some of them came down here for breakfast & told us it was General Iverson's command that was passing they having been cut off from the main body & were going to Augusta. At noon the whole command came up & Mr Friar came down to see us & told us Gen~ Wheeler was at the old field so we sent up at once and invited him to dine with us & he accepted our invitation & spent several hours with us. He says Kilpatrick joined the infantry at Louisville & has now advanced upon three roads leading to Augusta & thinks they may design marching upon that place or it may be that they have merely made that move to protect the infantry as they pass into the Savannah road. He says he has each bridge guarded over Brier Creek & hopes to be able to check their advance & earnestly hope he may succeed, but I do not believe it is Sherman's plan to go to Augusta. I think he will go towards Savannah as he can there operate with his fleet, should he be successful & will thus be able to accomplish more than by going to Augusta. I hope we will be able to keep him from Savannah though I doubt very much if we can hold the place as we have a small force in comparison to Sherman's immense army. I like Gen~ Wheeler very much indeed he is very pleasant & perfectly unassuming. Johnny Reynolds was with Genrl. Wheeler piloting him through the country & he also came to dinner; he says his Father has suffered very heavily, that the Yankees burnt up every thing but their dwelling & killed up all their stock & completely rifled the house. John Friar also dined with us & I was very glad to meet him again. Gano came down from Augusta this afternoon to join Wheeler. We had a note from Genrl Wheeler to-night saying he thought we might rest quietly as we were not likely to be disturbed by the Yankees.

Thursday, December 1, 1864

Every thing has been quiet to-day, our forces still at the old field & the Yankees remaining in camp. Genrl Wheeler's forces have thrown up fortifications at Brier creek & have prepared to burn the bridge should the Yankees attempt to cross & follow him up, he has sent back some of his forces already beyond the bridge. We did not sleep last night notwithstanding the note we had from General Wheeler, it was decidedly the most anxious night I have spent & we sat up the entire night. Genrl Wheeler had sent Dr Ward to stay here all night & carry dispatches from here on to Waynesboro should it be necessary & we felt so anxious we could not sleep, knowing the Yankees were not more than five miles from us & fearing they might advance & we knew if they should come upon us we would suffer for having Dr Ward here. It was the longest night I ever spent & I was delighted when daylight came. We had a visit from Dr Francis this morning, a brother of brother Jim & a very pleasant gentlemen, he is Division surgeon with the rank of Major. We begged him to stay & dine with us but he said he felt anxious to return to his command as he did not know but what they might move. He told us that General Wheeler had a fine opportunity of capturing

Kilpatrick the day after the Yankees were here, that he sent around a force in front of the enemy to burn the bridge at Buckhead creek but they failed to get there in time & thus the Yankees got away, he says we were pressing them very closely just there & as it was ran old Kilpatricks' hat off & would certainly have captured them had the bridge been burnt. I heard afterwards during the day, from some of our soldiers that General Iverson was the one sent to destroy the bridge & they all said he was a great coward & supposed he was afraid of the bullets I think he ought certainly to be court-martialed, I am not surprised to hear it of him however for any man that treated his wife as he did cannot make a good Soldier. Gano left to-day for Augusta as his horse was sick but says he will be back again in a few days. I cannot realize that this is the first day of winter, the air is more like Spring, soft & balmy. We have been blessed in having warm weather during the last week & I feel very thankful that such has been the case as we have been very much exposed. I feel so unsettled I cannot do any thing,

SKIRMISH AT ROCKY CREEK CHURCH

Dec. 2, 1864. Baird's division, 14th Corps, marching on the left of Gen. Sherman's army in support of Kilpatrick's cavalry division, which was enroute to burn the bridges over Brier Creek, NE of Waynesboro, reached Rocky Creek about 10:00 A.M. after skirmishing steadily with elements of Wheeler's cavalry for several miles. Here near the church, Baird found Wheeler posted on the east bank. The 74th Indiana Infantry attacked across the creek while other units crossed upstream and flanked out the defenders, who then fell back slowly to protect Waynesboro.

but wander about from place to place, & talk to our Soldiers as they pass trying to find out all the news from the enemy.

Friday, December 23, 1864

We hear today the dreadful news that Savannah has fallen, it is indeed a great blow to us, but I am not surprised to hear it as I feared we could not hold it. I am afraid Charleston & Augusta will both fall now, but pray that God may not allow them to gain so strong a foothold in this part of the country. I trust in him & leave everything in his hands knowing that what happens will be for our good.

Sunday, December 25, 1864

The greeting of "Merry Christmas" seems like a mockery, now, while there is so much trouble and suffering in our midst & I have not had the heart to give utterance to it today. What a striking contrast between this Christmas & those that were spent in former years; then it was a time of merry making, a time of joyful reunion when we were all gathered together in our happy home; now it is a season of sadness as it only recalls those joyous days that are gone, never more to return, as loved ones with us then, have passed away to meet with us again no more on earth & the brightest of our circle fallen by the hand of a savage & merciless foe. I have been thinking all day of the contrast between this & last Christmas, my darling was with me then & we were very happy together, & now there are many hundred miles between us, and many anxious hours do I spend in being separated from him, which is increased each day as I fail to hear from him, but I trust in God and pray that he will watch over and protect him from all dangers, disease and accident and yet bring us together again. God has been most merciful unto us and my heart is full of gratitude and thankfulness for all the blessings he has given me and above all do I thank him for having spared the life of my precious husband and child. Last Christmas a large party was assembled at dear old Ivanhoe and we had a happy time together and I remember so well how much pleasure the children had in receiving their presents from the Christmas tree; three of that party have since passed away, Charlie McCay, and dear little Lizzie and Clara. They are spending a happy Christmas in heaven for they are all bright angels in that peaceful and happy home.

I have had pleasure today in witnessing the happiness of my little darling. As soon as he opened his eyes this morning he called for his stocking and was perfectly wild with delight when he opened it and saw all the gifts from "Santa Claus," and exclaimed "oh! Mammer ain't Santa Taus a dood old man." I do wish Charlie could have seen him as I know it would have given him so much pleasure. I gave Millie the marbles aunty sent him, and he was delighted and they have been a great source of amusement to him. I regret we had not church to attend today but Mr. Porter did not come down, though we could not have gone to Waynesboro at any rate as it has been raining more or less all day. I have been suffering too with a headache and was unable to have Sunday school this afternoon. I hoped I would have a letter from my darling today but was disappointed I do feel so anxious to hear from him and Johnny since the Franklin fight but trust God has spared their precious lives. I commenced a letter to Charlie today but was unable to finish it as my head ached me so much. Bud, John and Johnny Davis left for Augusta this morning and I sent Lizzy and Lucy their little presents and sent some money to Ria. Though the retrospection today has been full of sadness, still I have not forgotten the many blessings left to us & trust I feel grateful for all God's merciful goodness & kindness unto us.

Sunday, January 1, 1865

We enter today upon another year, 1864 has passed away, carrying with it much of sorrow and sadness. It has indeed been a most eventful year, and the latter half of 1864 will always be remembered as the dark days in the history of this war for "southern rights." God grant the latter half of 1865 may be the brightest days and that er'e the close of the year we may be a free and independent nation. What a multitude of events are crowded into the last year and how sad the retrospection! Many brave and noble hearts have been hushed in death, many bright and happy homes laid waste by the invading foe and our own loved state almost a perfect wilderness! 1865 is ushered in with gloom and sadness and finds us still a suffering people, our political troubles are gathering thick and fast around us, everything is looking as dark and gloomy as possible and our country bleeding from every pore. The day however is bright and beautiful and I trust it may be ominous of a bright future and that God may deliver us out of the hands of our enemies. He overrules all things and ordereth all things alright and will do what is best for us which is an unspeakable comfort. I have blessings and mercies for which to return thanks and trust I am not unmindful of God's goodness to me, he has dealt most kindly and mercifully with me and has been specially gracious during the year that has passed; while many loved ones have been called away, and many too of our own family, he has spared the life of my precious husband and child and for this above all earthly blessings do I thank God. I deserve only his everlasting wrath for all the sins I have committed against, both my sins of omission and commission are very great and I lead a most profitless life and fall far short of my duty both to my neighbors and my God, but I shall endeavor henceforth, with God's help, to discharge my duties more faithfully and pray that he may be with me and help me to live more for him than I've ever done before. It was a great disappointment to me not being able to go to church this morning but we had no way. I had Sunday school this afternoon and my scholars recited good lessons and sang all their hymns beautifully. I have a great deal of pleasure in teaching them, it is the happiest hour of the week to me and I enjoy teaching them and strive to have the glory of my heavenly father in view and hope my own soul is profited by the exercises.

The Fall of Savannah, Georgia

REBELS EVACUATING SAVANNAH. DEC 20 64

Tuesday night, December 20, 1864, the forces under Gen. Hardee evacuated the city of Savannah, Ga. The Regulars were withdrawn from the works about eleven o'clock, and I will never forget passing through the city which was sealed. Doors were being knowcked down, guns were firing in every direction, the bullets flying over and around us. Women and children screaming and rushing in every direction. All combined made it a night never to be fortgotten by them who witnessed it. We finally reached the river where a string of rice barges strung end to end formed a bridge for us to cross on. The bridge was a poor makeshift, but the army succeeded in crossing it. While crossing the bridge, our way was lighted up by the burning of the Confederate gunboats and other vessels lying in the Savannah River. Sad to look at, but at the same time made a beautiful picture on the water. After the army had crossed, the barges were cut loose and destroyed.

W.H. Andrews
1st Sergeant, Company M
1st Georgia Infantry Regiment

Incidents of the fighting at Aiken

FEBRUARY 11, 1865

I WAS A MEMBER OF COMPANY I, 5TH GEORGIA CAVALRY, MADE UP FROM THE MEN OF OLD EFFINGHAM COUNTY, AND AT THE TIME WAS BUT NINETEEN YEARS OLD. After a lapse of nearly sixty years, my memory may not be exactly correct in all details, and if any of my comrades should criticise what I have written as to its correctness, I will not be offended.

After the fall of Savannah, in late December, 1864, our regiment, the 5th Georgia Cavalry, Anderson's Brigade, Wheeler's Corps, was stationed across the Savannah River from the city in South Carolina, to prevent the Yankee troops from making inroads and depredations on the country folk. However, as Sherman marched up through the State, we followed on, fighting Kilpatrick's cavalry daily, and when Sherman ordered him to Graniteville, S. C, and Augusta, Ga., to destroy the cotton stored there, our regiment was then in the lower part of the State. One night our Colonel Bird was ordered to effect a march of some sixty miles and report to General Wheeler at Aiken the next evening at six o'clock for important service. Immediately we took up the march, and reported in due time, having reached the vicinity of Aiken about dark. We were ordered to dismount and lie in line of battle, without even striking a match to cook anything and with but little opportunity to forage for our jaded horses. We privates did not know what was up, but just before the dawn we were marched to a position on the road leading into Aiken, the one Kilpatrick was expected to travel en route to Augusta. General Wheeler was trying to entrap him and capture his whole force. This ruse, no doubt, would have worked well but for the extra enthusiasm of an Alabama regiment ("Yellow-bammers").

My recollection is that we were formed into a hollow square, leaving one side open, through which Kilpatrick, would have to march. Of course, he was unaware of our presence. The Alabama regiment guarding the entrance on both sides was ordered not to fire a gun until the entire force had passed through, as the first shot would be a signal for a general engagement. However, when not more than half of Kilpatrick's troops had passed, some part of the Alabama boys opened fire and thus precipitated a general engagement, subjecting Wheeler's men to firing from both front and rear, instead of letting us close in on all four sides. However, we came near to getting Kilpatrick; captured a number of officers of high rank and quite a lot of his equipage, and drove him back to Sherman without accomplishing his purpose, thus saving Augusta and Graniteville and vast stores of cotton. Quite a number of the enemy were killed and wounded, and we suffered some severe losses ourselves.

General Wheeler did not think it wise to follow Kilpatrick farther that night, so, camping on the battle field, he awaited the morning to see that he had completely thwarted the attempt to reach Augusta. After caring for the wounded and burying the dead, we resumed the march, following Sherman on through the Carolinas to the last fight at Bentonville.

W.D. Morgan
Savannah, Georgia

SOUTH CAROLINA

Lexington • Columbia

Aiken
Johnson's Turnout
Windsor • Williston
Augusta

Salkahatchie River
Savannah River
South Carolina Railroad
Edisto River
River's Bridge

GEORGIA

Charleston
Fort Sumter

Fort Pulaski

0   25
MILES   Savannah

Hagan's Brigade
First Baptist Church
92nd Ill.
9th Ohio
Aiken
To Johnson's Turnout
9th Michigan
40th Ohio
10th Wisc.

SHOWDOWN AT AIKEN
February 10 – 13, 1865
Kilpatrick's route   Wheeler's route

Appomattox
APRIL 9-12, 1865

A CEREMONY TOOK PLACE AT APPOMATTOX COURT HOUSE. FEDERAL TROOPS FORMED ALONG THE PRINCIPAL STREET TO AWAIT THE FORMAL LAYING DOWN OF BATTLE FLAGS AND ARMS BY THE CONFEDERATES. Gen. Joshua Chamberlain of Maine described it: "On they come, with the old swinging route step and swaying battleflags. In the van, the proud Confederate ensign.... Before us in proud humiliation stood the embodiment of manhood; men whom neither toils and sufferings, nor the fact of death, nor disaster, nor hopelessness could bend from their resolve; standing before us now, thin, worn, and famished, but erect, and with eyes looking level into ours, waking memories that bound us together as no other bond." As the bugle sounded the Federal line shifted to the marching salute of carry arms. Gen. Gordon, riding heavy in spirit, saw the salute, whirled on his horse, dropped the point of his sword to the boot toe and ordered carry arms--"honor answering honor." And then the battle-worn colors of the regiments were folded and laid down until the Federal colors were against the sky. Memories, tears, victory, defeat blended into one.

—Compiled from the writings of
Joshua Chamberlain

Federal Soldiers who performed on EOF the last duties at Appomattox. A detail of the 26th Michigan handed out paroles to the surrendered confederates.

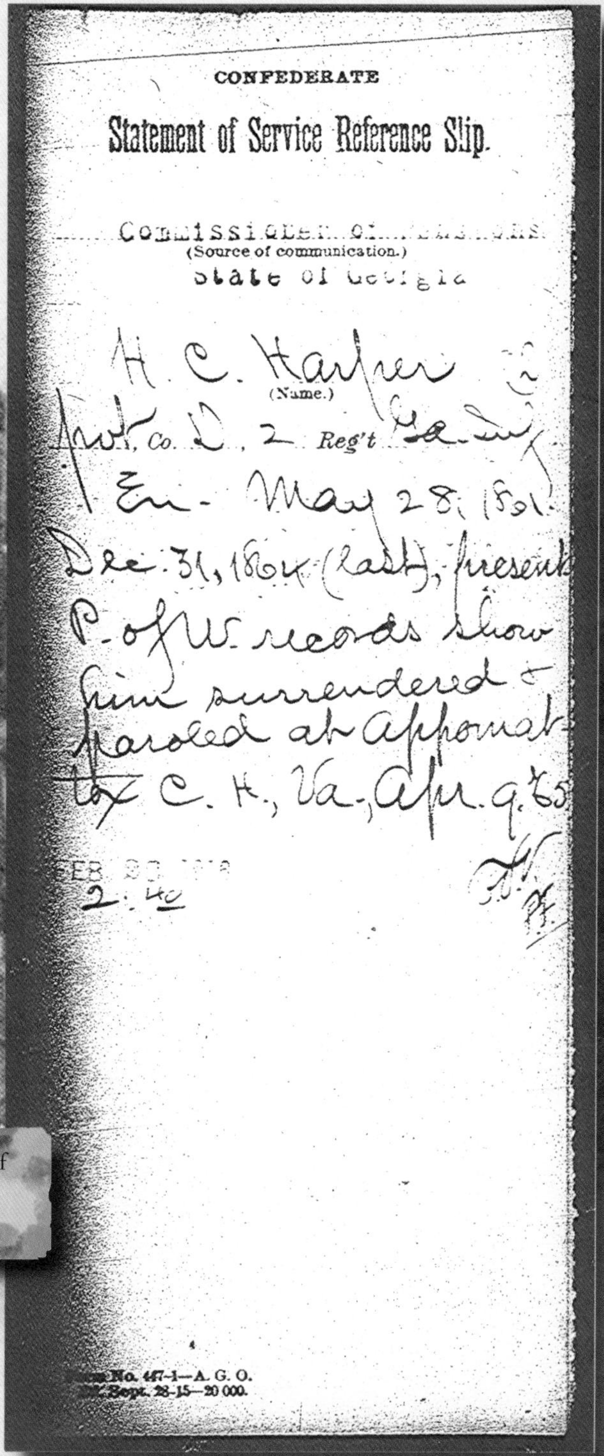

Service records of Private H.C. Harper of
Company D, 2nd GA Infantry CSA
National Archives, Washington, DC.

CONFEDERATE

Statement of Service Reference Slip.

Commissioner of Pensions
(Source of communication.)
State of Georgia

H. C. Harper
(Name.)

Pvt. Co. D. 2 Reg't Ga. Inf.

En. May 28, 1861.

Dec. 31, 1864 (last), present.

P. of W. records show
him surrendered +
paroled at Appomat-
tox C. H., Va., Apr. 9, '65

FEB 20 1918
2.40

Form No. 447-1—A. G. O.
Sept. 28-15—20 000.

Tuesday, April 18th, 1865

The painful rumors of Gen'l Lee's surrender have proven true. His army is surrounded and will be obliged to capitulate. Our cause is lost and who can tell the amount of that loss. Oh would that it had been otherwise. "Vae victis"* will now be the cry. May God in his mercy show the "silver lining" to this dark cloud and bring good out of seeming evil.

James E. Harper

Home Sweet Home

How well I can appreciate it after four years service. Four of the best years of my life thrown away. At the same time, I have no regrets to offer. I believed I was right and acted accordingly. I have tried to make a good soldier and perform all duties required of me, but since the war is ended will try and be a good a citizen for Uncle Sam as I was a soldier for the Confederacy.

W.H. Andrews
8th GA. Infantry Regiment

*Woe to the Vanquished

Entrance to Waverly Plantation, Waynesboro, Georgia.

MUSTER ROLL

COMPANY A, 2ND REGIMENT
BANKS COUNTY "BANKS COUNTY GUARDS"

Aerial, J. M. -- Private - April 20, 1861. Wounded in arm Gettysburg, Pennsylvania July 2, 1863. Roll for December 31, 1864, last on file, shows him present ★ Aerial, S. A. -- Private - November 21, 1861. Killed, Wilderness, Virginia May 6, 1864 ★ Allan, James Charlton -- Musician - April 20, 1861. Wounded. Appointed Sergeant Major, 11th Regiment, Georgia Cavalry, November 1863. Wounded and captured, Waynesboro, Georgia June 22, 1864. Released, Pt. Lookout Maryland June 22, 1865 ★ Allan, Robert -- 2nd Lieutenant - April 20, 1861. Died, fever, at Mrs. Foster's home near Manassas, Virginia, October 14, 1861 ★ Allen, Henry -- Private - April 20, 1861. Discharged, disability, May 25, 1862. Died Banks County, Georgia1862 ★ Allen, James H. -- Private - April 20, 1861. Discharged, disability, Richmond, Virginia October 18, 1861 ★ Andrews, James E. -- Private - April 20, 1861. Died, measles, General Hospital, Farmville, Virginia April 6, 1862 ★ Andrews, N. P. -- Private - April 20, 1861. Discharged, disability, Savannah, Georgia July 23, 1861 ★ Andrews, William J. (or J. W.) -- Private - April 20, 1861. Surrendered, Appomattox, Virginia April 9, 1865 ★ Ash, John R. -- Private - July 10, 1861. Killed, Gettysburg, Pennsylvania July 2, 1863 ★ Ash, William McCracken -- Private - April 20, 1861. Elected Ensign June 21, 1861; Jr. 2nd Lieutenant June 24, 1861. Resigned April 20, 1862 ★ Ayres, Obediah W. (or Ayers) -- Enlisted as a private, Company B, 15th Regiment, Georgia Infantry, July 14, 1861. Transferred to Cu. A, 2nd Regiment, Georgia Infantry, June 28, 1863. Roll for December 31, 1864, last on file, shows him present ★ Boling, McKinney M. -- Private - July 10, 1861. Transferred to Company H, 34th Regiment, Georgia Infantry, May 12, 1862. Severely wounded and captured, Baker's Creek, Mississippi May 16, 1863. Admitted to Prison Hospital, Baker's Creek, Mississippi May 17, 1863. No later record ★ Boling, Nathaniel S. -- Enlisted as a private, Company H, 34th Regiment, Georgia Infantry, March 26, 1863. Captured, Vicksburg, Mississippi July 4, 1863; and paroled there July 8, 1863. Transferred to Company A, 2nd Regiment, Georgia Infantry, August 1, 1864. Captured, Fort Harrison, Virginia September 29, 1864. No later record ★ Boling, William J. -- Private - April 20, 1861. Killed, 2nd Manassas, Virginia August 28, 1862 ★ Borders, Stephen L. -- Private - April 20, 1861. Appears last on roll for October 31, 1861. No record of transfer. Enlisted as a private in Company H, 34th Regiment, Georgia Infantry, May 12, 1862. Captured at Vicksburg, Mississippi July 4, 1863, and paroled there July 8, 1863. Captured near Nashville, Tennessee December 16, 1864. Received at Louisville, Kentucky January 2, 1865, and at Camp Chase, Ohio January 4, 1865. No later record ★ Bray, Benjamin -- Private - April 20, 1861. Appointed 1st Sergeant August 1, 1861. Appears last on roll for October 31, 1861 ★ Brewer, John W. -- Appointed 2nd Sergeant of Company A, 24th Regiment, Georgia Infantry, August 24, 1861. Transferred to Company A, 2nd Regiment, Georgia Infantry, March 1, 1863. Appointed Corporal. Surrendered, Appomattox, Virginia April 9, 1865 ★ Brewer, Joseph H. -- 3rd Sergeant - April 20, 1861. Appointed 1st Sergeant April 2, 1862. Elected 2nd Lieutenant April 26, 1862; 1st Lieutenant July 2, 1863. Surrendered, Appomattox, Virginia, April 9, 1865 ★ Brock, S. T. -- Private - April 20, 1861. Killed at Wilderness, Virginia May 6, 1864 ★ Brock, W. H. -- Private - April 20, 1861. Surrendered, Appomattox, Virginia April 9, 1865 ★ Brock, W. K. -- Private - April 20, 1861. Appointed 2nd Corporal. Surrendered, Appomattox, Virginia April 9, 1865 ★ Brown, Thomas J. -- Private - April 20, 1861. Died of measles at Brunswick, Georgia June 23, 1861 ★ Bullington, John L. -- Private - April 20, 1861. Wounded on picket duty, Manassas, Virginia November 1861. Died, wounds, in camp near Centreville, Virginia December 4, 1861 ★ Busch, Peyton E. (or Bush) -- Private - April 20, 1861. Discharged, disability, November 13, 1861 ★ Cagle, Henry -- Private - June 1, 1863. Captured, Gettysburg, Pennsylvania July 2, 1863. Exchanged, Boulware's & Cox's Wharves, James River, Virginia February 20, 1865 ★ Candler, Daniel Gill -- Captain - April 20, 1861. Resigned, disability, April 20, 1862. Made application for appointment as Post Quartermaster June 25, 1863. Born in Columbia County, Georgia in 1812. Died at Gainesville, Georgia

October 14, 1887 ★ Carr, William Henry -- Private - April 20, 1861. Appointed Corporal; Sergeant. Killed, Malvern Hill, Virginia July 1, 1862 ★ Carson, Thomas L. -- Private - July 27, 1861 Contracted chronic diarrhea in service. Leg disabled on march from Centreville to Richmond, Virginia March 1862. Sick in hospital December 3, 1864. Born April 7, 1843. Died Franklin County, Georgia February 22, 1925 ★ Chapman, James W. -- Private - April 20, 1861. Appointed Sergeant. Killed, Malvern Hill, Virginia July 1, 1862 ★ Chapman, M. N. -- Private - April 20, 1861. Injured on railroad at Petersburg, Virginia 1863. Absent on Surgeon's certificate of disability December 31, 1864 ★ Charlton, William W. -- 1st Lieutenant - April 20, 1861. Elected Captain April 20, 1862; Major July 2, 1863. Resigned January 15, 1864. Appointed "Com." of the 9th Congressional District of Georgia to pay claims, etc. December 3, 1864 ★ Chastain, H. S. -- Private - April 20, 1861. Surrendered, Appomattox, Virginia April 9, 1865 ★ Chastain, James B. -- 2nd Corporal - April 20, 1861. Wounded, 2nd Manassas, Virginia, August 30, 1862. Roll for December 31, 1864, last on file, shows him present ★ Chastain, John W. -- 4th Sergeant - April 20, 1861. Discharged account of chronic rheumatism December 7, 1861. Enlisted as a private, Company H, 34th Regiment, Georgia Infantry, 1863. Lost two fingers, Baker's Creek, Mississippi, May 16, 1863. Surrendered Greensboro North Carolina April 26, 1865 ★ Church, B. F. -- Private - April 20, 1861. Discharged, disability, Richmond, Virginia January 8, 1862 ★ Clarke, Henry F. -- Private - April 20, 1861. Appointed Sergeant. Captured, Mossy Creek, Tennessee January 22, 1864. Transferred from Rock Island, Illinois for exchange March 2, 1865. Paroled, Augusta, Georgia May 18, 1865 ★ Cox, J. T. -- Private - April 20, 1861. Surrendered, Appomattox, Virginia April 9, 1865 ★ Crocker, Josephus M. -- Private - July 10, 1861. Discharged, disability, 1861 ★ Crosby, Andrew -- Private - July 10, 1861. Appears last on roll for October 31, 1861 ★ Daniel, W. A. -- Private - April 20, 1861. Admitted to Chimborazo Hospital # 1, Richmond, Virginia March 19, 1862. Returned to duty April 5, 1862. No later record ★ Davis, Adrian -- Private - April 20, 1861. Discharged, disability, Richmond, Virginia October 18, 1861 ★ Dodd, Thomas R. -- Private - April 20, 1861. Appears last on roll for October 31, 1861 ★ Doyle, William Turner -- 1st Sergeant - April 20, 1861. Transferred to Company E, August 1, 1861. No later record ★ Duncan, Charles C. -- Private - April 20, 1861. Appointed Sergeant. Wounded, Gettysburg, Pennsylvania July 2, 1863. Roll for December 31, 1864, last on file, shows him present ★ Elliott, C. N. -- Private - April 20, 1861. Surrendered, Appomattox, Virginia April 9, 1865 ★ Elliott, Gaston G. -- Private - April 20, 1861. Appointed Corporal. Wounded in left arm and abdomen, Malvern Hill, Virginia July 1, 1862. Died, wounds, Chimborazo Hospital # 4, Richmond, Virginia July 6, 1862 ★ Estes, Martin Van Buren -- Private - April 20, 1861. Transferred to Company D, 44th Regiment, Georgia Infantry, June 1862. Appointed 3rd Sergeant; Sergeant. Elected Major July 1862. Wounded, Spotsylvania, Virginia May 10, 1864; Fort Steadman, Virginia March 25, 1865. Captured, High Bridge, Virginia April 6, 1865. Released, Newport News, Virginia June 15, 1865 ★ Estes, Obediah N. -- Enlisted as private in Company C, 18th Regiment, Georgia Infantry, April 30, 1861. Transferred to Company A, 2nd Regiment, Georgia Infantry, August 12, 1861. Died, typhoid fever, Richmond, Virginia September 15, 1861 ★ Forbis, Green B. -- Private - April 20, 1861. Wounded, Yorktown, Virginia April 5, 1862; 2nd Manassas, Virginia August 30, 1862. Severely wounded in leg, Chickamauga, Georgia September 19, 1863. Home on wounded furlough close of war ★ Forbis, Green J. -- Private - July 10, 1861. Discharged, disability, May 14, 1862 ★ Forbis, Thomas V. -- Private - April 20, 1861. Wounded, Malvern Hill, Virginia July 1, 1862. Leg permanently disabled, Gettysburg, Pennsylvania July 2, 1863. Home on wounded furlough close of war ★ Galey, S. D. -- Private - April 20, 1861. Left Savannah, Georgia for Homer, Georgia July 25, 1861. No later record ★ Griffin, Z. C. -- Private - April 20, 1863. Received by Provost Marshal General, Washington, D. C., from City Point, Virginia, a Confederate deserter, April 12, 1865. Took oath of allegiance to U. S.

Government and furnished transportation to Chattanooga, Tennessee April 1865 ★ Grubbs, G. W. -- Private - April 20, 1861. Appears last on roll for October 31, 1861 ★ Harris, Nathaniel -- Private - April 20, 1861. Admitted to Chimborazo Hospital #5, Richmond, Virginia May 25, 1862. Transferred to Camp Winder Hospital, Richmond, Virginia June 27, 1862. Killed while on furlough, Homer, Georgia, November, 1862 ★ Headen, Elisha P. -- Private - April 20, 1861. Discharged May 12, 1862 ★ Headen, William E. -- Private - April 20, 1861. Admitted to Chimborazo Hospital #2, Richmond, Virginia November 15, 1861. Transferred to 24th St. Georgia Hospital November 24, 1861. No later record ★ House, W. P. -- Private - April 20, 1861. Wounded, Chickamauga, Georgia September 19, 1863. Surrendered, Appomattox, Virginia April 9, 1865 ★ Hughes, Thomas J., Jr. -- Private - April 20, 1861. Transferred to Regimental Band. Wounded, Malvern Hill, Virginia July 1, 1862. Surrendered, Appomattox, Virginia April 9, 1865 ★ Kelley, Benjamin R. -- See Company H ★ King, William W. -- Private - January 1, 1863. Captured, Fort Harrison, Virginia September 29, 1864. Paroled, Pt. Lookout, Maryland March 17, 1865. Received, James River, Virginia for exchange March 19, 1865 ★ Maxey, A. N. -- Private - April 20, 1861. Surrendered, Appomattox, Virginia April 9, 1865 ★ McCullum, Robert E. S. (or McCollom) -- Private - July 10, 1861. Discharged, disability, Richmond, Virginia September 23, 1861. Enlisted as a private, Company A, 24th Regiment, Georgia Infantry, January 15, 1862. Discharged, disability, October 14, 1862 ★ McDonald, D. A. -- Private - April 20, 1861. Discharged, Richmond, Virginia October 21, 1861 ★ McDonald, J. P. -- Private - July 27, 1861. Wounded, Malvern Hill, Virginia July 1, 1862. Surrendered, Appomattox, Virginia April 9, 1865 ★ McDonald, John C. -- Private - April 20, 1861. Died prior to November 19, 1862 ★ McDonald, Martin Luther -- 1st Corporal - April 20, 1861. Discharged, disability, October 31, 1861. Elected Jr. 2nd Lieutenant, Company H, 34th Regiment, Georgia Infantry, May 12, 1862; 2nd Lieutenant April 1, 1863. Captured, Vicksburg, Mississippi, July 4, 1863, and paroled there July 8, 1863. Resigned account of tuberculosis January 21, 1864. Born Banks County, Georgia March 14, 1843. Died Banks County, Georgia, November 4, 1923 ★ McEntire, W. C. -- Private - April 20, 1861. Elected 2nd Lieutenant November 12, 1861. Appointed Assistant Surgeon, 2nd Regiment, Georgia Infantry, Received pay on January 2, 1865. No later record ★ McKie, Andrew S. -- Private - April 20, 1861. Killed, Malvern Hill, Virginia July 1, 1862 ★ McKie, Frank L. -- Private - April 20, 1861. Surrendered, Appomattox, Virginia April 9, 1865 ★ McKie, Samuel J. -- Private - April 20, 1861. Died near Athens, Georgia June 10, 1863 ★ McKie, Thomas C. -- Private - April 20, 1861. Wounded, Chickamauga, Georgia September 19, 1863. Died, wounds, October 1, 1863 ★ McMillan, James M. -- Private - April 20, 1861. Discharged, overage, Richmond, Virginia October 19, 1861 ★ Moore, David C. -- Private - April 20, 1861. Captured, Mossy Creek, Tennessee January 22, 1864. Exchanged. Surrendered, Appomattox, Virginia April 9, 1865 ★ Morris, David S. -- Private - July 10, 1861. Captured, Mossy Creek, Tennessee January 22, 1864. Died, pneumonia, Rock Island, Illinois March 19, 1864 ★ Morris, Henry M. -- 3rd Corporal - April 20, 1861. Sick Richmond, Virginia hospital October 31, 1861. Died, disease, 1861 ★ Morris, Richard V. -- Private - August 7, 1861. Transferred to Company H, 34th Regiment, Georgia Infantry, and appointed 5th Sergeant May 12, 1862. Appointed 1st Sergeant May 16, 1863. Surrendered, Greensboro, North Carolina April 26, 1865 ★ Moseley, Milton M. -- Jr. 2nd Lieutenant - April 20, 1861. Resigned June 24, 1861. Enlisted as a private, Company A, 24th Regiment, Georgia Infantry, August 24, 1861. Elected 1st Lieutenant, Company B, 3rd Battalion, Georgia Sharpshooters June 8, 1863. Captured, Wilderness, Virginia May 4, 1864. Released, Fort Delaware, Delaware June 16, 1865 ★ Moss, N. H. -- Private - April 20, 1861. Discharged, disability, Richmond, Virginia September 28, 1862 ★ Murray, B. R. (or B. K.) -- Private - August 7, 1861. Died, camp fever, Manassas, Virginia September 16, 1861 ★ Owen, A. W. -- Private - April 20, 1861. Appointed 4th Corporal January 20, 1862. Captured, Gettysburg, Pennsylvania July 3, 1863. Transferred from Fort Delaware, Delaware to Pt. Lookout, Maryland 1863, and died there January 27, 1864 ★ Owen, John W. -- Private - April 20, 1861. Appointed 1st Sergeant 1861. Elected 1st Lieutenant April 2, 1862; Captain January 15, 1864. Surrendered, Appomattox, Virginia April 9, 1865 ★ Owen, W. C. -- Private - April 20, 1861. Died, measles, 1861 ★ Parker, John W. -- Private - April 20, 1861. Roll for December 31, 1864, last on file, shows him present ★ Peak, G. A. -- Private - April 20, 1861. Wounded, Sharpsburg, Maryland September 17, 1862. Transferred to Company B, 15th Regiment, Georgia Infantry, and appointed Musician July 28, 1863. Transferred to Company E, October 14, 1864. Received, Washington, D. C., a Confederate deserter, and furnished transportation to New York City

April 12, 1865 ★ Perry, John H. -- Private - July 10, 1861. Died in service ★ Pruitt, Samuel W. -- Private - April 20, 1861. Transferred to 24th Regiment, Georgia Infantry, and appointed Captain and Assistant Quartermaster September 21, 1861. Dropped for failure to give bond February 24, 1862 ★ Pruitt, W. B. -- Private - April 20, 1861. Absent without leave June 30-December 31, 1864 ★ Ray, James F. -- 4th Corporal - April 20, 1861. Discharged, disability, January 20, 1862. Appointed 1st Sergeant, Company E, 16th Battalion, Georgia Cavalry, May 14, 1862. Elected 2nd Lieutenant September 20, 1862; Captain, Company H, September 19, 1863. Transferred to Company H, 13th Regiment, Georgia Cavalry, May 2, 1864. Captured and paroled, Athens, Georgia, May 8, 1865 ★ Richards, J. C. -- Private - April 20, 1861. Appointed 1st Sergeant 1863. Surrendered, Appomattox, Virginia April 9, 1865 ★ Richards, W. P. -- Private - August 7, 1861. Died, camp fever, Richmond, Virginia September 19, 1861 ★ Richey, James Alfred -- 2nd Sergeant - April 20, 1861. Discharged June 1862. Enlisted as a private, Company E, 16th Battalion, Georgia Cavalry, February 4, 1863. Transferred to Company G, 13th Regiment, Georgia Cavalry, May 2, 1864. Captured Andersonville, South Carolina May 3, 1865 ★ Rucker, Wiley -- Private - April 20, 1861. Admitted to Moore Hospital, Danville, Virginia with rheumatism December 24, 1861. Died in Virginia prior to July 17, 1862 ★ Scales, Moore H. -- Private - April 20, 1861. Died, disease, Moore Hospital, Danville, Virginia February 10, 1862 ★ Simmons, M. N. -- Private - April 20, 1861. Discharged, disability, October 28, 1862 ★ Simmons, Willis M. -- Private - April 20, 1861. Paroled, Augusta, Georgia May 25, 1865. ★ Slayter, J. B. (or Slayton) -- Private - July 10, 1861. Killed, Wilderness, Virginia May 6, 1864 ★ Slayton, Thomas N. -- Private - April 20, 1861. Appointed Sergeant. Surrendered, Appomattox, Virginia April 9, 1865. ★ Smith, Burgess -- Private - April 20, 1861. Paroled, Augusta, Georgia May 18, 1865 ★ Smith, James C. -- Private - July 10, 1861. Sick in Richmond, Virginia hospital October 31, 1861. No later record ★ Smith, Jasper -- Private - April 20, 1861. Captured, Gettysburg, Pennsylvania July 5, 1863. Paroled, DeCamp General Hospital, David's Island, New York 1863. Received, City Point, Virginia for exchange September 27, 1863. Roll for December 31, 1864, last on file, shows him absent without leave ★ Spencer, Absalam -- Private - July 10, 1861. Transferred to Company C, 18th Regiment, Georgia Infantry, August 16, 1861. Appears last on roll for October 2, 1861 ★ Ussery, G. John -- Private - 1864. Captured, Dorchester December 13, 1864. No later record ★ Vaughn, W. R. -- Private - July 10, 1861. Wounded in Virginia. Surrendered, Appomattox, Virginia April 9, 1865 ★ Walker, D. L. -- Private - September 21, 1861. Captured, Fort Harrison, Virginia September 30, 1864. Released, Pt. Lookout, Maryland June 6, 1865 ★ Walker, H. A. -- Private - June 20, 1861. Died, measles, Fredericksburg, Virginia 1862 ★ Walker, J. B. -- Private - June 20, 1861. Elected Jr. 2nd Lieutenant August 5, 1862. Roll for December 31, 1864, last on file, shows him present ★ Waters, Moses -- Private - August 7, 1861. Roll for October 31, 1861, shows him present. Enlisted as a private, Company G, 1st Regiment, Georgia State Troops, February 11, 1863. On special service March 1864. Roll dated May 31, 1864, last on file, shows him present ★ Waters, Powell A. -- Private - August 7, 1861. Elected 2nd Lieutenant April 28, 1862. Resigned disability, July 1, 1862. Enlisted as a private, Company G, 1st Regiment, Georgia State Troops, March 25, 1863. Appointed 1st Sergeant May 11, 1863; 1st Lieutenant June 23, 1863; Captain ★ White, Alexander -- Private - June 20, 1861. Transferred to Company B, 15th Regiment, Georgia Infantry, May 12, 1862; to Company G. 1st Regiment South Carolina Cavalry January 30, 1863. Appointed Corporal. Roll for December 31, 1864, last on file, shows him present ★ Willbanks, S. D. -- Private - April 20, 1861. Wounded, Gettysburg, Pennsylvania July 2, 1863. Surrendered, Appomattox, Virginia April 9, 1865 ★ Willbanks. J. R. -- Private - July 27, 1861. Paroled, Burkeville, Virginia April 17, 1865 ★ Williamson, George D. -- Private - May 7, 1861. Died, measles, Brunswick, Georgia June 14, 1861 ★ Wood, John H -- Private - April 20, 1861. Appointed Sergeant. Captured near Knoxville, Tennessee December 3, 1863. Died, disease, Rock Island, Illinois January 29, 1864 ★ Wood, Thomas J. -- Private - April 20, 1861. Died May 12, 1862 ★ Young, David C. -- Private - June 20, 1861. Discharged, disability, Richmond, Virginia October 10, 1861.

COMPANY B, 2ND REGIMENT
MERIWETHER COUNTY "JACKSON BLUES"

Allbright, Jacob D. -- Private - July 12, 1861. Surrendered, Appomattox, Virginia April 9, 1865 ★ Baker, Morrill C. -- Private - July 12, 1861. Wounded in skirmish October 29, 1864. Absent, wounded, December 31, 1864. No later record ★ Barnes, Edwin S. -- Private - August 26, 1861. Appears last on roll for October 31, 1861 ★ Beavers, William H. -- Private - July 12, 1861. Wounded, Fort Harrison, Virginia September 29, 1864. Surrendered, Appomattox, Virginia April 9, 1865 ★ Beck, James W. -- 3rd Sergeant - July 12, 1861. Appears last on roll for October 31, 1861 ★ Bishop, Asa W. -- Private - July 12, 1861. Discharged, disability, October 19, 1861 ★ Bowden, John M. (or Bowdin) -- Private - August 26, 1861. Wounded and captured, Fort Harrison, Virginia September 29, 1864. Paroled, Pt. Lookout, Maryland and transferred to Atkin's Landing, Virginia for exchange March 17, 1865. Received Boulware's Wharf, James River, Virginia March 19, 1865 ★ Braswell, Isaac L. -- Private - August 26, 1861. Absent, sick, Richmond, Virginia October 31, 1861. No later record. ★ Braynon, John J. -- Private. Captured, Murfreesboro, Tennessee January 4, 1863. Appears on roll of prisoners of war paroled and delivered at City Point, Virginia, with remarks, not to be found, sick. Roll is indorsed "Rec'd. February 18, 1863." No later record ★ Breakfield, William A. -- Private - July 12, 1861. On detached duty, wagoner, October 31, 1861. No later record ★ Brown, Monroe W. -- Private - July 12, 1861. Discharged, disability, November 4, 1861. Enlisted as a private, Company K, 55th Regiment, Georgia Infantry, May 3, 1862. Discharged account of tuberculosis February 28, 1863 ★ Bullock, Henry E. -- Private - July 12, 1861. Died with measles near Manassas, Virginia September 5, 1861 ★ Bush, John P. -- Private - 1863. Surrendered, Tallahassee, Florida May 10, 1865. Paroled, Albany, Georgia May 18, 1865 ★ Bussey, Samuel H. -- Private - August 26, 1861. Captured at Sharpsburg, Maryland September 19, 1862. Exchanged, Aiken's Landing, Virginia November 10, 1862. Roll for December 31, 1864, last on file, shows him present ★ Bussey, W. H. -- Private - August 11, 1862. Surrendered, Appomattox, Virginia April 9, 1865 ★ Campbell, Nicholas Charter -- Private - July 12, 1861. Absent, sick, in Richmond, Virginia October 31, 1861. Elected Jr. 2nd Lieutenant of Company F, 12th Regiment, Georgia State Guards Cavalry (Robinson's), August 8, 1863. Mustered out February 10, 1864 ★ Carroll, Asbury N. -- Private - July 12, 1861. Died with fever near Richmond, Virginia October 14, 1861 ★ Catenhead, William P. -- Private - July 12, 1861. Appears last on roll for October 31, 1861 ★ Clements, Stephen D. -- 1st Lieutenant - July 12, 1861. Elected Captain of Company F, 41st Regiment, Georgia Infantry, July 26, 1862. Wounded at Perryville, Kentucky October 8, 1862. Captured at Vicksburg, Mississippi July 4, 1863, and paroled there July 6, 1863. Detailed on General Court Martial December 23, 1863. Severely wounded at Atlanta, Georgia July 22, 1864. At home on wounded furlough close of war. (Born in Georgia in 1832.) ★ Cole, W. -- Private. Surrendered, Appomattox, Virginia April 9, 1865 ★ Connell, Joseph B. -- Private - August 26, 1861. Wounded. Surrendered, Appomattox, Virginia April 9, 1865 ★ Corley, John H. -- Private - July 12, 1861. Absent, sick, Richmond, Virginia October 31, 1861. No later record ★ Corley, William T. -- Private - July 12, 1861. Appears last on roll for October 31, 1861 ★ Crowder, James -- Private - July 12, 1861. Absent, sick, Richmond, Virginia October 31, 1861. Davis, Roan H. -- Private - July 12, 1861. Discharged, disability, Richmond, Virginia January 8, 1862 ★ Davis, William T. -- Private - July 12, 1861. Appears last on roll for October 31, 1861 ★ Ellis, Henry J. -- Private - March 1, 1864. Captured, Darbytown Road, Virginia October 7, 1864. Exchanged, Pt. Lookout, Maryland February 13, 1865. Home on furlough close of war ★ Ellis, Robert N. -- Private - July 12, 1861. Discharged, Richmond, Virginia October 20, 1861. Reenlisted October 2, 1863. Surrendered, Appomattox, Virginia April 9, 1865 ★ Ferrell, Micajah -- 2nd Sergeant - July 12, 1861. Wounded,

Wilderness, Virginia May 6, 1864. Admitted to Richmond, Virginia hospital May 8, 1864. No later record ★ Florence, James W. -- Private - July 12, 1861. Appears last on roll for October 31, 1861 ★ Florence, William M. -- Private - July 12, 1861. Roll for December 31, 1864, last on file, shows him present. No later record. Born in 1839. Died, Thomaston, Georgia March 11, 1936 ★ Florence, William T. -- Private - July 12, 1861. Appointed Sergeant. Left arm disabled, Chickamauga, Georgia September 19, 1863. Elected 1st Lieutenant, Company A, 4th Regiment, Georgia Reserve Infantry May 10, 1864. Appointed Adjutant May 28, 1864. Roll for December 31, 1864, last on file, shows him present ★ Franklin, James Cicero -- Private - July 12, 1861. Elected 2nd Lieutenant April 28, 1862. Killed at Gettysburg, Pennsylvania July 1, 1863 ★ Freeman, Robert A. S. -- Private - July 12, 1861. Appointed 1st Sergeant August 19, 1861. Elected 1st Lieutenant April 28, 1862; Captain January 15, 1864. Surrendered, Appomattox, Virginia April 9, 1865 ★ Fuller, Jones Calhoun. -- Private - July 12, 1861. Captured, Wilderness, Virginia May 6, 1864. Released, Pt. Lookout, Maryland May 1865 ★ Funderburk, Andrew J. -- Private - July 12, 1861. Surrendered, Appomattox, Virginia April 9, 1865 ★ Funderburk, David -- Private - September 17, 1861. Captured, Fort Harrison, Virginia September 29, 1864. Released, Pt. Lookout, Maryland June 27, 1865 ★ Funderburk, Henry C. -- Private - July 12, 1861. Absent, sick, Richmond, Virginia October 31, 1861. No later record ★ Funderburk, John R. -- Private - July 12, 1861. Captured, Fort Harrison, Virginia September 29, 1864. Received, Boulware's & Cox's Wharves, James River, Virginia for exchange March 19, 1865 ★ Gill, Joseph S. -- Private - July 12, 1861. Died, measles, Richmond, Virginia hospital November 6, 1861 ★ Goodwin, Wesley Pierce -- Private - July 12, 1861. Wounded and disabled, Wilderness, Virginia May 6, 1864. Captured, Macon, Georgia April 1865 ★ Granger, Isham W. -- Private - July 12, 1861. Wounded 1862. Leg or arm amputated, Culpeper, Virginia hospital September 27, 1862. Sent to General Hospital September 28, 1862. No later record ★ Grier, Alfred S. -- Private - July 12, 1861. Appears last on roll for July 30, 1861 ★ Griffin, Robert H. -- Private - July 12, 1861. Wounded, Wilderness, Virginia May 6, 1864. No later record ★ Griggs, Rhodum -- Private - July 12, 1861. Absent, sick, Richmond, Virginia hospital October 31, 1861. No later record ★ Grimsley, Colsby R. -- Private - August 26, 1861. Appears last on roll for October 31, 1861 ★ Hall, Joseph Y. -- Private - July 12, 1861. Died in hospital November 14, 1861 ★ Hancock, Henry L. -- Private - July 12, 1861. Wounded, Cold Harbor, Virginia June 3, 1864. Surrendered, Appomattox, Virginia April 9, 1865 ★ Harmon, Thomas J. -- Private - July 12, 1861. Discharged, disability, Richmond, Virginia August 10, 1861 ★ Harris, William Terrell -- Captain - July 12, 1861. Elected Major April 28, 1862; Lieutenant Colonel September 17, 1862. Killed at Gettysburg, Pennsylvania July 2, 1863 ★ Head, William J. -- 2nd Corporal - July 12, 1861. Absent, sick, Richmond, Virginia October 31, 1861. No later record ★ Hightower, Joseph D. -- Private - July 12, 1861. Captured. Paroled, Warrenton, Virginia September 29, 1862. No later record ★ Hinchcliti, Fred J. (or Hinscliffe) -- Musician - July 12, 1861. Absent, sick, Richmond, Virginia October 31, 1861. No later record ★ Hines, Elias D. -- Private - July 12, 1861. Absent, sick, Richmond, Virginia hospital October 31, 1861. No later record ★ Jackson, Joseph Baldwin -- Private - July 12, 1861. Appears last on roll for October 31, 1861 ★ Jones, J. J. A. -- Private. Appointed 3rd Sergeant. Surrendered, Appomattox, Virginia April 9, 1865 ★ Jones, James O. -- Private - July 12, 1861. Surrendered, Appomattox, Virginia April 9, 1865 ★ Jones, John T. -- Private - July 12, 1861. Discharged, disability, October 24, 1861 ★ Jones, Josiah -- Private - July 12, 1861. Died, Richmond, Virginia September 20, 1861. Buried there Hollywood Cemetery ★ Jordan, Henry W. -- Private - July 12, 1861. Appears last on roll for October 31, 1861 ★ Key, John G. W. -- Private - July

12, 1861. Discharged, disability, December 23, 1861. Enlisted as a private Company K, 55th Regiment, Georgia Infantry, May 3, 1862 ★ Key, John H. -- Private - July 12, 1861. Died, typhoid pneumonia, Camp Georgia near Manassas, Virginia February 19, 1862 ★ Lane, Morrill W. -- Private - July 12, 1861. Surrendered, Appomattox, Virginia April 9, 1865 ★ Leslie, Erasmus M. (or Lesley) -- Private - July 12, 1861. Absent, sick at Richmond, Virginia, October 31, 1861. No later record in this company. Enlisted as a private in (New) Company A, 60th Regiment, Georgia Infantry, May 10, 1863. Captured at Spotsylvania, Virginia May 20, 1864. Paroled at Elmira., New York March 10, 1865. Received at Boulware & Cox's Wharves, James River, Virginia for exchange, March 15, 1865. No later record ★ Lewis, Abner McC. -- 2nd Lieutenant - July 12, 1861. Elected Captain April 28, 1862. Wounded in leg, resulting in amputation, at Chickamauga, Georgia September 19, 1863. Elected Major January 15, 1864. Retired, disability, December 23, 1864 ★ Lewis, James F. -- Private - July 12, 1861. Elected 2nd Lieutenant July 1, 1863; 1st Lieutenant January 15, 1864. Captured at Fort Harrison, Virginia September 29, 1864. Released at Fort Delaware, Delaware June 17, 1865 ★ Matthews, W. H. -- Private - 1865. Paroled, Augusta, Georgia May 23, 1865 ★ McCord, Joseph -- Private - July 12, 1861. Absent, sick in Richmond Virginia hospital, October 31, 1861. No later record ★ McCord, Seaborn -- Private - July 12, 1861. Died, disease, November 1861 ★ Meachum, Joel C. -- 4th Sergeant - July 12, 1861. Appointed 1st Sergeant 1864. Wounded, Wilderness, Virginia and sent to General Hospital May 6, 1864. Roll for December 31, 1864, last on file, shows him absent, wounded ★ Middlebrooks, John -- Private - July 12, 1861. Surrendered, Appomattox, Virginia April 9, 1865 ★ Middlebrooks, Thomas J. -- Private - July 12, 1861. Appears last on roll for October 31, 1861 ★ Moore, Seaborn T. -- Private - 1862. Paroled, Augusta, Georgia May 20, 1865 ★ Moss, Abner M. -- Private - July 12, 1861. Appears last on roll for October 31, 1861 ★ Moss, Gabriel -- Private - July 12, 1861. Died, measles, Clay Street hospital, Richmond, Virginia September 5, 1861 ★ Mullins, John L. -- Private - July 12, 1861. Absent, sick, Richmond, Virginia October 31, 1861. No later record ★ Nelson, Joseph H. -- Private - July 12, 1861. Appointed Quartermaster Sergeant 1861. Surrendered, Appomattox, Virginia April 9, 1865 ★ Owen, James R. -- 1st Corporal - July 12, 1861. Wounded and disabled, Gettysburg, Pennsylvania July 2, 1863. Discharged, disability, May 4, 1864 ★ Paine, Thomas – Musician - July 12, 1861. Discharged, disability, August 21, 1861 ★ Parham, Robert S. -- Jr. 2nd Lieutenant - July 12, 1861. Discharged 1862. Detailed near Richmond, Virginia to superintend farm and provide supplies for army May 1862. Enlisted in Company ?, Regiment, Georgia Militia 1864. Discharged April 1865 ★ Peavy, David J. -- Private - July 12, 1861. Wounded. Malvern Hill, Virginia July 1, 1862. Died, wounds, Richmond, Virginia July 17, 1862 ★ Perdue, Hilliard J. -- Private - July 28, 1861. Surrendered, Appomattox, Virginia April 9, 1865 ★ Perdue, Isham C. -- Private - July 12, 1861. Captured, West Point, Georgia April 16, 1865. Sent to Military Prison, Macon, Georgia, April 23, 1865 ★ Phillips, John H. -- Private - July 12, 1861. Absent, sick, Richmond, Virginia hospital October 31, 1861. No later record ★ Phillips, Nathan -- Private - July 12, 1861. Discharged, disability, January 10, 1862 ★ Poane, Robert H. -- 3rd Corporal - July 12, 1861. Discharged, disability, November 4, 1861 ★ Radney, James S. -- Private - July 12, 1861. Appointed Sergeant. Wounded and permanently disabled, Sharpsburg, Maryland, September 17, 1862. Absent, wounded December 31, 1864 ★ Robinson, John H. -- Private - July 12, 1861. Absent, sick, Richmond, Virginia October 31, 1861. No later record ★ Rosser, Robert P. -- Private - July 12, 1861. Absent, sick, Richmond, Virginia October 31, 1861. No later record ★ Rosser, Willis D. -- Private - July 12, 1861. Absent, sick, Richmond, Virginia October 31, 1861. Died September 18, 1862 ★ Savage, M. D. -- Private - August 26, 1861. Discharged, disability, October 19, 1861 ★ Seay, George W. (or -- See) -- Private - July 12, 1861. Surrendered, Appomattox, Virginia April 9, 1865 ★ Sewell, John Asbury -- Private - July 12, 1861. Discharged, disability, at Richmond, Virginia December 24, 1861. Enlisted as a private in Company B, 1st Regiment, Georgia Cavalry, March 4, 1862. Roll for December 31, 1864, last on file, shows him present. No later record ★ Sewell, John R. -- Private - July 12, 1861. Killed June 20, 1864 ★ Sheffeld, William W. -- Private - July 12, 1861. Wounded and disabled. On wounded furlough February 17, 1865 ★ Shepherd, Richard H. -- Private - July 12, 1861. Roll for December 31, 1864, last on file, shows him present ★ Simmons, John D. -- Private - July 12, 1861. Surrendered, Appomattox, Virginia April 9, 1865 ★ Simmons, Vincent C. -- Enlisted as a private in Company E, 28th Regiment, Georgia Infantry, March 10, 1864. Transferred to Company B, 2nd

Regiment, Georgia Infantry, November 16, 1864. Wounded in 1865. Captured, Petersburg, Virginia hospital April 3, 1865, and died there of wounds April 24, 1865 ★ Sims, Sterling A. -- Private - July 12, 1861. Discharged, Richmond, Virginia August 23, 1861 ★ Sims, William S. -- Private - July 12, 1861. Wounded and permanently disabled, Garnetts Farm, Virginia June 27, 1863. Absent, wounded, December 31, 1864 ★ Smith, John T. -- Private - July 12, 1861. Died, disease; Orange Court House, Virginia March 24, 1862 ★ Smith, Lewis T. -- See private, Company F ★ Smith, Robert Allen -- Private - July 12, 1861. Died, disease, Richmond, Virginia July 28, 1862 ★ Snelson, Abner J. -- Private - July 12, 1861. Discharged, spinal disease, Centreville, Virginia November 27, 1861 ★ Stanford, William -- Private - July 12, 1861. Absent, sick, Richmond, Virginia hospital October 31, 1861. No later record ★ Staples, Abraham D. -- Private - July 12, 1861. Appears last on roll for October 31, 1861 ★ Stephenson, William H. -- 1st Sergeant - July 12, 1861. Discharged, disability, Richmond, Virginia August 19, 1861 ★ Stevens, William H. -- Private - July 12, 1861. Arm disabled, Fort Harrison, Virginia September 29, 1864. Absent, wounded, December 31, 1864 ★ Tillman, James M. -- Private - August 26, 1861. Surrendered, Appomattox, Virginia April 9, 1865 ★ Vardeman, J. E. -- Private. Surrendered, Appomattox, Virginia April 9, 1865 ★ Vardeman, M. Bishop -- Private - July 12, 1861. Surrendered, Appomattox, Virginia April 9, 1865 ★ Watson, J. L. -- Private. Surrendered, Appomattox, Virginia April 9, 1865 ★ Westbrook, Bryan A. -- Private - July 12, 1861. Killed, Chickamauga, Georgia September 20, 1863 ★ Wheelus, John T. -- 4th Corporal - July 12, 1861. Appears last on roll for October 31, 1861 ★ Wheelus, Thomas A. -- Private - July 12, 1861. Died, Richmond, Virginia hospital December 10, 1861 ★ Willis, Henry W. -- Private - July 12, 1861. Appears last on roll for October 31, 1861 ★ Winslow, John Benjamin -- Private - July 12, 1861. Absent, sick, Richmond, Virginia October 31, 1861. No later record. Died in Manchester, Georgia, May 14, 1922 ★ Wooley, J. J. -- Private. Surrendered, Appomattox, Virginia April 9, 1865

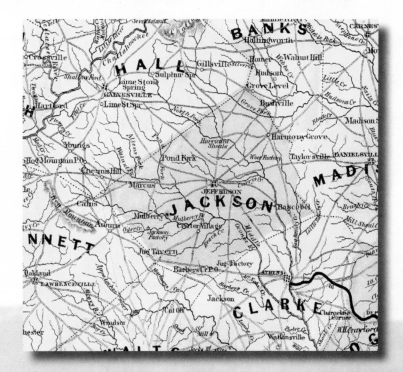

Company C, 2nd Regiment
Muscogee County "Semmes Guards"

Adams, Henry Y. -- Private - July 24, 1861. Died, Orange County Court House, Virginia January 19, 1862 ★ Aenchbacher, Gotlieb N. -- Private - July 24, 1861. Wounded, Chickahominy, Virginia June 27, 1862. Captured, Fort Harrison, Virginia September 29, 1864. Paroled, Pt. Lookout, Maryland 1865. Transferred to Aiken's Landing, Virginia for exchange March 17, 1865. Received, Boulware s & Cox's Wharves, James River, Virginia March 19, 1865 ★ Albright, Jacob Amos -- 1st Corporal - July 24, 1861. Wounded and permanently disabled, Chickahominy, Virginia June 27, 1862. On detail duty in hospital, account of disability, October 31, 1864-January 1, 1865 ★ Arnold, George W. -- Private - July 24, 1861. Wounded, Chickahominy, Virginia June 27, 1862. Surrendered, Appomattox, Virginia April 9, 1865 ★ Averitt, Jasper -- 4th Corporal - July 24, 1861. Appointed 1st Sergeant June 27, 1862. Surrendered, Appomattox, Virginia April 9, 1865 ★ Baker, Major A. -- Private - July 24, 1861. Discharged, under-age, October 21, 1861. Enlisted as a private, Company E, 31st Regiment, Georgia Infantry, November 13, 1861. Died, Camp Philips, Georgia March 19, 1862 ★ Barbour, William A. (or Barker) -- 3rd Corporal - July 24, 1861. Captured, Deep Bottom, Virginia September 25, 1864. Paroled, Pt. Lookout, Maryland and transferred to Aiken's Landing, Virginia for exchange, March 17, 1865. Received, Boulware s & Cox's Wharves, James River, Virginia March 19, 1865 ★ Biggers, J. W. -- Private - August 6, 1861. Wounded, Chickahominy, Virginia June 27, 1862. Surrendered, Appomattox, Virginia April 9, 1865 ★ Burks, John L. -- Private - July 24, 1861. Wounded, Garnett's Farm, Virginia June 27, 1862. On detail duty in Conscript Department in Georgia September 1863 to close of war ★ Cheney, William Melton -- Private - July 24, 1861. Wounded, Chickahominy, Virginia June 27, 1862. Surrendered, Appomattox, Virginia April 9, 1865 ★ Cooley, Charles W. -- Enlisted as a private in Company C, 46th Regiment, Georgia Infantry, March 4, 1862. Transferred to Company C, 2nd Regiment, Georgia Infantry, in exchange for E. P. Willis, February 11, 1863. Deserted August 1863 ★ Corbett, Mauger A. -- Private - July 24, 1861. Wounded in arm, resulting in amputation, Gettysburg, Pennsylvania July 2, 1863. In Columbus, Georgia hospital, wounded, close of war ★ Cowan, John R. -- Private - July 24, 1861. Captured, Deep Bottom, Virginia September 25, 1864. Paroled, Pt. Lookout, Maryland and transferred to Aiken's Landing, Virginia for exchange March 17, 1865 ★ Crouch, John Thomas -- Private - July 24, 1861. Killed, Chickahominy, Virginia June 27, 1862 ★ Davidson, Joseph W. -- Private - July 24, 1861. Wounded, Chickahominy, Virginia June 27, 1862. Died, wounds, July 2, 1862 ★ Deas, Nelson -- Private - July 5, 1864. Appears last on roll for August 30, 1864 ★ Dewberry, Seaborn H. -- Private - July 24, 1861. Admitted to Chimborazo Hospital #3, Richmond, Virginia May 11, 1862. Killed, Gettysburg, Pennsylvania July 1, 1863 ★ Dewberry, Thomas J. -- Private - July 24, 1861. Killed, Chickahominy, Virginia, June 27, 1862 ★ Douglass, D. Z. -- Private - 1864. Surrendered, Augusta, Georgia May 20, 1865 ★ Drake, Nathan B. -- Private - July 25, 1861. Discharged, disability, February 23, 1862 ★ Evans, Cornelius J. -- Private - July 24, 1861. Killed Chickahominy, Virginia June 27, 1862 ★ Fitts, J. F. -- Private - July 24, 1861. Admitted to Chimborazo Hospital #3, Richmond, Virginia November 27, 1861, and died there, pneumonia, December 13, 1861 ★ Fitzgerald, Seaborn D. -- Private - July 24, 1861. Wounded, Chickahominy, Virginia June 27, 1862. Died, wounds, July 1, 1862 ★ Flannagan, James Madison -- Private - July 24, 1861. Surrendered, Appomattox, Virginia April 9, 1865 ★ Foster, Frank B. -- Private - July 24, 1861. Died, typhoid pneumonia, January 30, 1862 ★ Gilbert, John -- Private - July 24, 1861. Discharged, disability, Centerville, Virginia November 27, 1861 ★ Gilbert, M. L. -- Private - July 24, 1861. Admitted to Chimborazo Hospital #1, Richmond, Virginia January 13, 1862. No later record ★ Green, Louis -- Private - July 24, 1861. Discharged, never having acquired a domicile, July 31, 1862 ★ Greenwood, Julius -- Private - July 24, 1861. Discharged, exempt from duty July 12, 1862 ★ Gresham, Marmaduke -- Private - July 24, 1861. Surrendered, Appomattox, Virginia April 9, 1865 ★ Hayden, A. P. (or Haden) -- Private - July 24, 1861. Admitted to Chimborazo Hospital #5, Richmond, Virginia with pneumonia March 15, 1862. Returned to duty April 21, 1862. Admitted to C. S. A. General Hospital, Charlottesville, Virginia with erysipelas April 26, 1864. Returned to duty May 3, 1864. Killed, Wilderness, Virginia May 6, 1864 ★ Henderson, J. N. -- Private - January 24, 1863. Surrendered, Appomattox, Virginia April 9, 1865 ★ Henry, W. B. -- Private - July 24, 1861. Discharged, disability, August 8, 1861 ★ Hill, H. H. -- Private - July 24, 1861. Killed September 1864 ★ Hill, Isaac Thomas -- Private - July 24, 1861. Elected Jr. 2nd Lieutenant April 28, 1862; 1st Lieutenant September 17, 1862. Captured, Gettysburg, Pennsylvania July 3, 1863. Received, Boulware's & Cox's Wharves, James River, Virginia for exchange March 22, 1865. ★ Hill, Robert G. -- 3rd Sergeant - July 24, 1861. Wounded, Gettysburg, Pennsylvania July 2, 1863. Killed, Fort Harrison, Virginia September 29, 1864 ★ Hollifield, Theophilus (or Holyfield) -- Private - January 12, 1863. Absent without leave September 18, 1863 -January 1, 1865. No later record ★ Hopkins, J. B. -- Private - July 24, 1861. Appointed Sergeant. Killed, Wilderness, Virginia May 6, 1864 ★ Horton, J. F. -- Private - July 24, 1861. Captured, Suffolk, Virginia May 16, 1863. Exchanged, City Point, Virginia May 23, 1863. No later record ★ Howard, Robert N. -- 1st Lieutenant - July 24, 1861. -- See private, Company G ★ Jenkins, Benjamin C. -- Private - July 24, 1861. Roll for December 31, 1864, last on file, shows him present ★ Johnson, F. M. -- Private - January 17, 1863. Surrendered, Appomattox, Virginia April 9, 1865 ★ Kendrick, C. B. -- Private - July 24, 1861. Discharged, disability, October 21, 1861. Enlisted as a private, Company H, 54th Regiment, Georgia Infantry, May 12, 1862. Roll for February 29, 1864, last on file, shows him present ★ Kennedy, James R. -- Private - July 5, 1864. Captured near Richmond, Virginia September 25, 1864. Received, Boulware's & Cox's Wharves, James River, Virginia for exchange February 20-21, 1865 ★ Kennedy, John R. -- Private - July 24, 1861. Wounded, Chickahominy, Virginia June 27, 1862. Received pay February 17, 1865. No later record ★ Land, Joseph B. -- Private - July 24, 1861. Surrendered, Appomattox, Virginia April 9, 1865 ★ Lewis, William D. -- Private - July 24, 1861. Wounded and permanently disabled September 20, 1863. In hospital, wounded, close of war ★ Ligon, O. E. -- Private - July 24, 1861. Died, apoplexy, Camp Pine Creek, Virginia September 28, 1861 ★ Lynch, W. T. B. -- Private - July 24, 1861. Wounded, Chickahominy, Virginia June 27, 1862. Surrendered, Appomattox, Virginia April 9, 1865 ★ Lyons, David -- Private - July 24, 1861. Captured, Richmond, Virginia April 3, 1865. Released, Newport News, Virginia June 25, 1865 ★ Mallory, W. R. -- Private - July 24, 1861. Admitted to Chimborazo Hospital #1, Richmond, Virginia October 17, 1861. Transferred to 3rd Georgia Hospital. No later record ★ Martin, M. J. -- Private - July 21, 1862. Surrendered, Appomattox, Virginia April 9, 1865 ★ McCarty, James -- Private - July 24, 1861. Paroled, Augusta, Georgia May 20, 1865 ★ McCoy, Perkins W. -- 2nd Corporal - July 24, 1861. Surrendered, Appomattox, Virginia April 9, 1865 ★ McGehee, J. G. -- Private - July 24, 1861. Elected 2nd Lieutenant. Killed, Gettysburg, Pennsylvania July 2, 1863 ★ Mixon, George S. -- Private. Paroled Augusta, Georgia April 26, 1865 ★ Moore, S. D. -- Private - January 27, 1863. Discharged, disability, May 30, 1864 ★ Morley, James D. -- Private - July 24, 1861. Captured, Deep Bottom, Virginia September 25, 1864. Received, Boulware's & Cox's Wharves, James River, Virginia for exchange March 19, 1865 ★ Morris, William J. -- 2nd Sergeant - July 24, 1861. Surrendered, Appomattox, Virginia April 9, 1865 ★ Moseley, J. D. -- Private - July 24, 1861. Missing, Fort Harrison, Virginia September 29, 1864. No later record ★ Murrell, D. J. -- Private - July 24, 1861. Discharged, disability, December 21, 1861 ★ Nelms, R. N. -- Private - July 24, 1861. Killed, Wilderness, Virginia May 6, 1864 ★ Newman, James -- Private - July 24, 1861.

Wounded, Chickahominy, Virginia June 27, 1862. Died, wounds, July 1862 ★ Oliver, Henry -- Private - July 24, 1861. Wounded, Chickahominy, Virginia June 27, 1862. Surrendered, Appomattox, Virginia April 9, 1865 ★ Osteen, Isaac W. -- Private - July 24, 1861. Received at General Hospital at Danville, Virginia August 13, 1862. Returned to duty October 10, 1862. No later record ★ Parker, Alex J. -- 1st Sergeant - July 24, 1861. Killed, Chickahominy, Virginia June 27, 1862 ★ Parker, T. H. -- Private - March 4, 1862. Appears last on roll for August 31, 1864 ★ Parker, West W. -- Private - January 12, 1863. Surrendered, Appomattox, Virginia April 9, 1865 ★ Parks, John H. -- Private - January 26, 1863. Wounded at Gettysburg, Pennsylvania July 2, 1863. Absent without leave December 31, 1864 ★ Patterson, J. W. B. -- Private - July 24, 1861. Appointed Corporal. Wounded in finger at Chickahominy, Virginia June 27, 1862. Admitted to Charlottesville, Virginia hospital account of wounds, September 3, 1862. Died at Lynchburg, Virginia October 6, 1862, and buried there in Confederate Cemetery. No. 2, 1st Line, Lot 181. Taken up 22nd October and sent to Columbus, Georgia, 5 o'clock Christian's Factory ★ Patterson, John J. -- Private. Wounded January 21, 1862; Chickahominy, Virginia June 27, 1862. Discharged account of wounds 1863 ★ Paxton, David Marion -- Private - September 2, 1861. Captured at Gettysburg, Pennsylvania July 2, 1863. Paroled at Point Lookout, Maryland in 1865. Exchanged at James River, Virginia February 14-15, 1865. Born in Henry County, Georgia February 15, 1836. Died in 1905. Buried at Locust Grove, Georgia ★ Pitts, Samuel R. -- 1st Sergeant. -- See private, Company G ★ Pitts, Sterling G. -- Private - July 24, 1861. Severely wounded at Chickahominy, Virginia June 27, 1862. Sent to Christian and Lea's Hospital, Richmond, Virginia June 1862. Admitted to Chimborazo Hospital #2, at Richmond, Virginia with debility. March 24, 1863. Returned to duty April 2, 1863. No later record ★ Price, Irwin -- Private - January 23, 1863. Surrendered, Appomattox, Virginia April 9, 1865 ★ Ramey, S. H. -- See private, Company K ★ Redd, William, Jr. -- Jr. 2nd Lieutenant - July 24, 1861. -- See private, Company G ★ Redding, James P. -- Private - July 24, 1861. Appointed Corporal. Admitted to Chimborazo Hospital #3, at Richmond, Virginia March 7, 1862. Furloughed to end of enlistment April 8, 1862 ★ Renfroe, John G. -- Private - July 24, 1861. Died, typhoid pneumonia, Camp Georgia near Manassas, Virginia January 28, 1862 ★ Roby, William -- Private - July 24, 1861. Wounded, Chickahominy, Virginia June 27, 1862. Lost finger October 1864. Captured, Richmond, Virginia April 3, 1865, and paroled there May 5, 1865 ★ Russell, Charles R. -- 2nd Lieutenant - July 24, 1861. -- See private, Company G ★ Shepherd, William S. -- Captain - July 24, 1861. -- See private, Company G ★ Short, James N -- Private - July 24, 1861. Captured, Fort Harrison, Virginia September 30, 1864. Exchanged March 17, 1865 ★ Short, Jasper -- Private - July 24, 1861. Admitted to Richmond, Virginia hospital October 24, 1861. Discharged, disability, Richmond, Virginia October 29, 1861 ★ Terrell, Charles F. -- Private - August 26, 1862. Captured, Front Royal, Virginia September 20, 1864. Exchanged. Roll for January 1, 1865, last on file, shows him present ★ Tucker, Ferdinand N. -- Private - July 24, 1861. Wounded, Spotsylvania, Virginia May 12, 1864. On wounded furlough in Russell County, Alabama January 1, 1865 ★ Walker, John A. -- Private - January 1863. Died in hospital March 21, 1863 ★ Wamble, Thomas S. -- 4th Sergeant - July 24, 1861. Surrendered, Appomattox, Virginia April 9, 1865 ★ Weems, J. A. -- Private - July 21, 1861. Transferred to Company G, 1861. Absent, sick, Richmond, Virginia October 25, 1861 ★ Wells, Jerome -- Private - April 1864. Captured near Dallas, Georgia, May 26, 1864. Died, peritonitis, Rock Island, Illinois July 2, 1864 ★ Willis, Edward Payson -- Private - July 24, 1861. Wounded, Chickahominy, Virginia June 27, 1862. Transferred to Company C, 46th Regiment, Georgia Infantry, in exchange for C. W. Cooley, February 11, 1863. Surrendered, Greensboro, North Carolina April 26, 1865. Born in Muscogee County, Georgia, April 21, 1841. Died in Midland, Georgia, July 2, 1923.

COMPANY D, 2ND REGIMENT
BURKE COUNTY "BURKE SHARPSHOOTERS"

Applewhite, W. W. -- Private - April 19, 1861. Sick in hospital June 30, 1861. No later record ★ Arrington, O. H. -- Private - April 19, 1861. Transferred to Regimental Band 1861. Appears last on roll for August 31, 1861 ★ Ashton, John D. -- Private - April 19, 1861. Elected Captain, Company D, 11th Battalion, Georgia Infantry March 4, 1862. Transferred to Company D, 47th Regiment, Georgia Infantry, as Captain May 12, 1862. Resigned October 14, 1862. Elected Captain, Company M, 4th Regiment, Georgia Cavalry, (Avery's). Captured, Chickamauga, Georgia September 19, 1863 (also shown as Summerville, Georgia September 10, 1863 and Lawrenceville, Georgia September 20, 1863.) Received, Military Prison, Louisville, Kentucky October 5, 1863. Forwarded to Johnson's Island, Ohio, October 13, 1863. Sent from Point Lookout, Maryland to Fort Delaware, Delaware June 25, 1864. Forwarded to Hilton Head, South Carolina August 20, 1864. Paroled, Charleston Harbor, South Carolina, December 15, 1864. Surrendered May 10, 1865. Paroled, Albany, Georgia May 17, 1865 ★ Ashton, W. W. -- Private - April 19, 1861. Transferred to Company D, 2nd Regiment Louisiana Infantry April 23, 1862. Appointed Sergeant. Surrendered, Appomattox, Virginia April 9, 1865 ★ Atterway, Thomas -- Private - September 2, 1862. Paroled, Augusta, Georgia May 18, 1865 ★ Barton, David -- Private - April 19, 1861. Surrendered, Appomattox, Virginia April 9, 1865 ★ Bates, John F. -- Private - April 19, 1861. Appointed 3rd Sergeant. Surrendered, Appomattox, Virginia April 9, 1865 ★ Bellfield, William -- Private - April 19, 1861. Appointed Musician. Captured, Farmville, Virginia April 6, 1865. Released, Pt. Lookout, Maryland June 23, 1865 ★ Blount, A. -- Private - April 19, 1861. Appointed Corporal. Transferred to Company I, Cobb's Legion Georgia Cavalry, September 4, 1863. On detail to procure horses September 19, 1864. No later record ★ Blount, S. W. -- Private - April 19, 1861. Paroled, Augusta, Georgia May 18, 1865 ★ Blount, T. E. -- Private - April 19, 1861. Captured, Gettysburg, Pennsylvania July 2, 1863. Died, pyemia, DeCamp General Hospital, David's Island, New York August 8, 1863 ★ Blount, W. A. -- Private - April 19, 1861. Transferred to Company ?, Cobb's Legion Georgia Cavalry, March 12, 1864. Surrendered, Greensboro, North Carolina April 26, 1865 ★ Bostwick, C. A. W. (or Bostick) -- Private - April 19, 1861. Absent without leave November 1864 -January 11, 1865 ★ Bostwick, F. C. (or Bostick) -- Private - May 30, 1861. Sick in Richmond, Virginia hospital May 30, 1862. No later record ★ Bragg, W. L. -- Private. Received pay from July 1st to 31st. No later record ★ Brazell, W. A. -- Private - April 19, 1861. Absent without leave, at home, January 11, 1865 ★ Burdell, Ferdinand Victor -- Private - May 9, 1861. Made application for appointment as Lieutenant of Artillery, C. S. A., or to a clerkship in one of the Government departments (no record found of his appointment to either position,) November 5, 1862. Transferred to Engineer Corps, Savannah, Georgia under General Hardee, September 11, 1862. Surrendered, Savannah, Georgia April 15, 1865. Died, Blythe, Georgia, April 9, 1925 ★ Burton, James G. -- 2nd Sergeant - April 19, 1861. Wounded. Absent, wounded, March 24, 1863 ★ Byne, Thomas A. -- 3rd Sergeant - April 19, 1861. Appears last on roll for June 30, 1861 ★ Carpenter, B. -- Private - June 12, 1861. At home, sick, June 30, 1861. No later record ★ Carter, E. A. -- Private - April 19, 1861. Discharged, disability, August 20, 1862 ★ Cole, John -- Musician - April 19, 1861. Transferred to Regimental Band 1861. Captured, Morristown, Tennessee January 11, 1864. Released, Rock Island, Illinois May 16, 1865 ★ Cox, G. H. -- Private - April 19, 1861. Appears last on roll for June 30, 1861 ★ Cox, V. F. -- Private - April 19, 1861. Appears last on roll for August 7, 1863 ★ Cox, W. R. -- Private - April 19, 1861. Appointed 1st Sergeant. Surrendered, Appomattox, Virginia April 9, 1865 ★ Davenport, T. E. -- Private - April 19, 1861. Captured, Tallahassee, Florida May 10, 1865. Paroled, Bainbridge, Georgia May 20, 1865 ★ Dickerson, W. H. -- Private - April 19, 1861. Elected 1st Lieutenant April 28, 1862; Captain July 1, 1862. Wounded in arm, resulting in amputation, Wilderness, Virginia May 6, 1864 ★ Dixon, Jeff, Jr. -- Private - April 19, 1861. Appears last on roll for June 30, 1861

★ Dye, Benjamin G. -- Private - April 19, 1861. Surrendered, Appomattox, Virginia April 9, 1865 ★ Dye, W. A. -- Private - May 30, 1864. Roll for December 31, 1864, last on file, shows him absent with leave ★ Elliott, T. D. -- Private - April 19, 1861. Sick in hospital June 30, 1861. No later record ★ Frost, J. E. -- Private - April 19, 1861. Absent without leave, at home, December 31, 1864 ★ Fryer, B. A. -- Private - April 19, 1861. Admitted to Chimborazo Hospital #2, Richmond, Virginia November 11, 1861. Transferred to 3rd Georgia Hospital November 12, 1861. No later record ★ Fryer, John B. -- Private - April 19, 1861. Appears last on roll for June 30, 1861 ★ Godbee, C. G. -- Private - May 25, 1861. Roll for June 30, 1861 shows him present. No later record in this company. Enlisted as a private, Company C, 32nd Regiment, Georgia Infantry, May 12, 1862. Roll for October 31, 1864, only roll on file, shows him present ★ Godbee, H. V. -- Private - April 19, 1861. Absent, sick, Savannah, Georgia June 30, 1861. No later record ★ Godbee, L. F. -- Private - April 19, 1861. Roll for December 31, 1864, last on file, shows him absent without leave ★ Graves, Andrew -- Private - April 19, 1861. Roll for December 31, 1864, last on file, shows him present ★ Green, Charles A. -- Private - April 19, 1861. Transferred to Regimental Band May 15, 1861. Captured, Farmville, Virginia April 6, 1865. Released, Newport News, Virginia June 15, 1865 ★ Green, Joseph Isaiah -- Private - April 19, 1861. Wounded in finger, resulting in amputation, Malvern Hill, Virginia July 1, 1862. Surrendered, Appomattox, Virginia April 9, 1865 ★ Hankinson, R. A. -- Private - April 19, 1861. Killed, Wilderness, Virginia May 6, 1864 ★ Harper, H.C. (Henry Clay) private-May 28, 1861. Wounded Malvern Hill. Treated and released from Chimborazo Hospital, Richmond, Virginia. Surrendered Appomattox, Virginia April 9, 1865. ★ Harper, J.E. Private-April 19, 1861. Discharged due to typhoid fever March 1862 and returned to Augusta, Georgia. Enlisted 27th Georgia Infantry Regiment February 1864. Surrendered at Greensboro, North Carolina April 1865. See diary of James E. Harper deposited at Richmond County Historical Society. ★ Harrold, William -- Private - May 15, 1861. Sick in hospital June 30, 1861. No later record.Holmes, William R. -- Captain - April 19, 1861. Elected Lieutenant Colonel April 28, 1862. Killed, Sharpsburg, Maryland September 17, 1862 ★ Hudson, J. H. -- Private - April 19, 1861. Home on furlough December 31, 1864. No later record ★ Hughes, C. J. -- 3rd Corporal - April 19, 1861 ★ Hughes, James W. -- Private - April 19, 1861. Roll for December 31, 1864, last on file, shows him absent without leave ★ Hurst, G. W. -- Private - April 19, 1861. Elected 2nd Lieutenant December 18, 1862. Killed, Gettysburg, Pennsylvania July 2, 1863 ★ Jenkins, T. B. B. -- Private - May 15, 1861. Appears last on roll for June 30, 1861 ★ Jones, Charles M. -- Private - May 25, 1861. Elected 1st Lieutenant and Ensign, 2nd Regiment, Georgia Infantry, July 2, 1864. Surrendered, Appomattox, Virginia April 9, 1865 ★ Jones, James P. -- Private - April 19, 1861. Discharged by order of Secretary of War October 19, 1861 ★ Lewis, S. E. A. -- 2nd Corporal - April 19, 1861. Admitted to Moon Hospital, General Hospital #1, Danville, Virginia with fever December 29, 1861. No later record. ★ Lewis, William H. H. -- Private - May 15, 1861. Admitted to Chimborazo Hospital #2, Richmond, Virginia with diarrhea May 18, 1862. Returned to duty May 29, 1862. No later record ★ Lorenz, John P. -- Private - April 19, 1861. Discharged never having acquired a domicile July 17, 1862 ★ Lovett, C. C. -- Private - April 19, 1861. At home, sick, June 30, 1861. No later record ★ Lovett, W. H. H. -- Private - April 19, 1861. Appointed 5th Sergeant 1861. Surrendered, Appomattox, Virginia April 9, 1865 ★ Lynch, Benjamin T. -- Private - May 15, 1861. Wounded in Virginia December 10, 1864. Died, wounds, December 13, 1864 ★ Lynch, H. N. -- Private - June 20, 1861. Died, Fredericksburg, Virginia hospital September 3, 1861 ★ Marsher, H. P. -- Private - May 24, 1861. Appears last on roll for June 30, 1861 ★ Martin, Jerry -- Private - May 15, 1861. Surrendered, Appomattox, Virginia April 9, 1865 ★ McElhinny, W. L. -- Private - April 19, 1861. Absent on business June 30, 1861. No later record ★ McNorrill, K P. (or McNowell) -- Private - April 19, 1861. Discharged, disability, November 1, 1861 ★ Milledge, Richard Habersham -- Private - June 1, 1861. Transferred to Milledge's Battery, Georgia Light Artillery, 1862. Appointed Sergeant. Roll for October 1864, last on file, shows him present. At Danville, Virginia en route to command close of war ★ Miller, T. P. -- Private - April 19, 1861. Absent without leave January 11, 1865 ★ Mills, H. V. -- Private - April 19, 1861. At home, sick, June 30, 1861. No later record ★ Oakman, Clifford -- Private - May 20, 1861. At home, sick, June 30, 1861. Enlisted as a private, Company C, 48th Regiment, Georgia Infantry, February 28, 1862. Paroled, Richmond, Virginia April 1865. Died, Valdosta, Georgia ★ Oakman, Raymond -- Private - April 19, 1861. Received pay for commutation of rations May 27, 1863. Killed, Gettysburg, Pennsylvania July 1863 ★ Oakman, Robert Harper -- Jr. 2nd Lieutenant - April 19, 1861. Retired at reorganization April 28, 1862 ★ Oglesby, J. J. -- Private - June 12, 1861. Appears last on roll for June 30, 1861 ★ Packard, D. W. -- Private - April 19, 1861. Elected 2nd Lieutenant August 1, 1862. Killed, 2nd Manassas, Virginia August 31, 1862 ★ Parker, Solomon -- Private - May 28, 1861. Received pay for commutation of rations for 86 days. March 27, 1863. No later record ★ Perkins, E. -- Private - April 19, 1861. Died at home June 19, 1861 ★ Perry, Henean H. -- 1st Sergeant - April 19, 1861. Sick in hospital June 30, 1861. No later record ★ Quinney, W. C. -- Private - May 28, 1861. Surrendered, Appomattox, Virginia April 9, 1865 ★ Rawls, H. -- Private - April 19, 1861. Wounded, 2nd Manassas, Virginia August 30, 1862. Leg amputated on battlefield, Manassas, Virginia September 3, 1862 ★ Reese, J. C. -- Private - April 19, 1861. Appears last on roll for June 30, 1861 ★ Reynolds, John W. -- 4th Corporal - April 19, 1861. Discharged, Richmond, Virginia, 1862 ★ Rind, W. M. -- Private - May 28, 1861. Appears last on roll for June 30, 1861 ★ Roberts, D. B. -- Private - April 19, 1861. Appears last on roll for June 30, 1861 ★ Roberts, G D -- Private - April 19, 1861. Appointed 2nd Corporal. Surrendered, Appomattox, Virginia April 9, 1865 ★ Roberts, T. E. -- Private. Surrendered, Appomattox, Virginia April 9, 1865 ★ Rogers, B. F. -- Private - April 19, 1861. Elected 2nd Lieutenant July 2, 1863; 1st Lieutenant 1864. Surrendered, Appomattox, Virginia April 9, 1865 ★ Sanders, William -- Private - September 24, 1863. Wounded in finger, resulting in amputation, Wilderness, Virginia May 6, 1864. Surrendered, Appomattox, Virginia April 9, 1865 ★ Sapp, George W. -- Private - April 19, 1861. Sick in hospital June 30, 1861. Captured in Virginia August 1, 1863. Exchanged 1864. Detailed by order Secretary of War to superintend farm, Burke County, Georgia, August 1864, and continued in that capacity to close of war ★ Sapp, John -- Private - May 15, 1861. Appears last on roll for June 30, 1861 ★ Sapp, Judson C. -- 4th Sergeant - April 19, 1861. Elected 2nd Lieutenant April 28, 1862; 1st Lieutenant July 1, 1862. Killed in Virginia August 1, 1863 ★ Sawtell, J. P. -- Private - April 19, 1861. Wounded 1863. Absent without leave, at home, December 31, 1864 ★ Skinner, U. -- Private - April 19, 1861. At home, sick, June 30, 1861. No later record ★ Skinner, William -- Private - April 19, 1861. At home, sick, June 30, 1861. No later record ★ Tabb, D. B. -- Private - April 19, 1861. Appointed Corporal. Roll for December 31, 1864, last on file, shows him absent without leave ★ Tabb, William -- Private - April 19, 1861. Roll for December 31, 1864, last on file, shows him absent without leave, supposed to have deserted ★ Tarver, E. -- Private - April 19, 1861. Surrendered, Appomattox, Virginia April 9, 1865 ★ Thompkins, William Augustus -- Private - April 19, 1861. Wounded, Wilderness, Virginia May 6, 1864. Admitted to Floyd House & Ocmulgee Hospitals, Macon, Georgia, with wound in right shoulder, followed by partial anchylosis May 9, 1864. On detail duty in Conscript Department in Georgia August 31, 1864. Paroled, Augusta, Georgia May 19, 1865 ★ Thompson, Walter A. -- 2nd Lieutenant - April 19, 1861. Elected Captain April 28, 1862. Killed, Malvern Hill, Virginia July 1, 1862 ★ Tipton, R. M. (or Typton) -- Private - April 19, 1861. Roll for December 31, 1864, last on file, shows him absent without leave, supposed to have deserted ★ Walker, R. A. -- Private - April 19, 1861. Appears last on roll for June 30, 1861 ★ Wallace, H. F. -- Private. Surrendered, Appomattox, Virginia April 9, 1865 ★ Wallace, Henry Allen -- Private - April 19, 1861. Roll for January 11, 1865, shows him present. No later record. (Born in Burke County, Georgia December 16, 1839. Died May 11, 1907.) ★ Wallace, N. S. -- Private - May 25, 1861. Appears last on roll for June 30, 1861 ★ Wallace, S. W. -- Private - April 19, 1861. Appointed 4th Sergeant April 28, 1862. Surrendered, Appomattox, Virginia April 9, 1865. ★ Wallace, Stiring C. -- Enlisted as a private, Company E, 2nd Regiment, 1st Brigade, Georgia State Troops, October 12, 1861. Discharged. Enlisted as a private, Company D, 2nd Regiment, Georgia Infantry, November 28, 1862. Wounded, Chickamauga, Georgia September 19, 1863; Winchester, Virginia September 19, 1864. Enlisted as a

private, 61st District, 7th Regiment 2nd Brigade, 1st Division, Georgia Militia, date not given ★ Ward, Charles A. -- Private - May 20, 1864. Died, chronic colitis, General Hospital #12, Greensboro September 16, 1864 ★ Ward, E. L. A. -- Private - April 19, 1861. Home on furlough January 11, 1865 ★ Watkins, J. R. -- Private - May 28, 1861. Surrendered, Appomattox, Virginia April 9, 1865 ★ Whitehead, John P. C. Jr. -- 1st Lieutenant - April 19, 1861. On furlough June 30, 1861. Appointed Brigade Inspector, 1st Division, 2nd Brigade Georgia State Troops, February 22, 1862 ★ Whitehead, W. D. -- 1st Corporal - April 19, 1861. Killed, Malvern Hill, Virginia July 1, 1862. Buried Hollywood Cemetery, Richmond, Virginia ★ Wilde, J. R. -- Private - June 20, 1861. Discharged August 10, 1861 ★ Woodward, Joseph W. -- Private - April 19, 1861. Discharged, Richmond, Virginia December 1861. Elected 1st Lieutenant, Company D, 52nd Regiment, Georgia Infantry, March 4, 1862; Captain August 20, 1862. Captured, Vicksburg, Mississippi July 4, 1863 and paroled there July 1863. Wounded, left arm permanently disabled, New Hope Church, Georgia May 25, 1864. In State Line Hospital, Jonesboro, Georgia close of war. (Born in Georgia, October 1, 1843. Died, Dahlonega, Georgia, June 6, 1922.) ★ Wray, James M. -- Private - April 19, 1861. On detail duty in Quartermaster Department, Oconic, Virginia December 31, 1864 ★ Wright, James R. -- Enlisted as a private in Company K, 26th Regiment, Georgia Infantry, May 29, 1861. Transferred to Company D, 2nd Regiment, Georgia Infantry, June 15, 1861. Appointed Regimental Musician 1861. Wounded in leg, resulting in amputation, July 5, 1864 ★ Youngblood, David Y. -- Private - April 19, 1861. Paroled, Farmville, Virginia April 11-12, 1865.

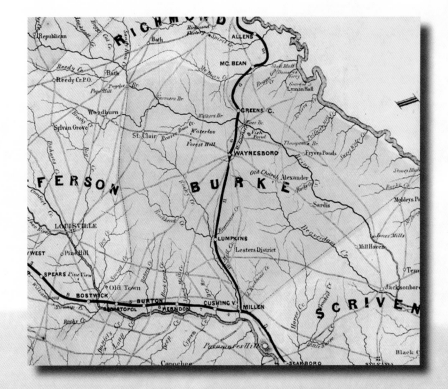

Company E, 2nd Regiment
Fannin County "The Joe Browns"

Addington, John S. -- Private - April 22, 1861. Appears last on roll for July 1, 1861 ★ Beard, James H. -- Private - April 22, 1861. Appears last on roll for July 1, 1861 ★ Beaver, Alfred M. -- Private - April 22, 1861. Absent without leave from September 19, 1863. Took oath of allegiance to U. S. Government, Chattanooga, Tennessee, March 29, 1864 ★ Beaver, Jesse R. -- Jr. 2nd Lieutenant - April 22, 1861. Resigned September 24, 1861 ★ Beaver, William J. -- Private - April 22, 1861. Surrendered, Appomattox, Virginia April 9, 1865 ★ Benton, J. S. -- Private. Surrendered, Appomattox, Virginia April 9, 1865 ★ Bivins, Thomas J. -- Private - April 22, 1861. Absent without leave April 15-December 31, 1864 ★ Bradley, A. L. -- Private - August 17, 1861. Absent without leave March 1-December 31, 1864 ★ Bradley, John M. -- Private - April 22, 1861. Died February 25, 1862 ★ Bradley, Samuel P. -- Private - April 22, 1861. Appears last on roll for July 1, 1861 ★ Brady, Enoch -- 3rd Sergeant - April 22, 1861. Died, fever, Savannah, Georgia June 16, 1861 ★ Brady, J. P. -- Private - March 28, 1864. Surrendered, Appomattox, Virginia April 9, 1865 ★ Brady, John W. -- Private - April 22, 1861. Roll for December 31, 1864, last on file, shows him present ★ Bramlett, Rufus -- Private - April 22, 1861. Took oath of allegiance to U. S. Government, Chattanooga, Tennessee, April 7, 1864 ★ Brendle, James P. -- Private - April 22, 1861. Captured, Fredericksburg, Virginia December 13, 1862. Paroled for exchange December 17, 1862. Absent without leave April 15-December 31, 1864 ★ Cabe, W. V. -- 4th Corporal - April 22, 1861. Appears last on roll for July 1, 1861 ★ Campbell, William A. -- Captain - April 22, 1861. Retired April 28, 1862 ★ Chastain, B. F. -- Private - May 9, 1861. Appears last on roll for July 1, 1861 ★ Chastain, Elisha -- Private - August 17, 1861. On detached duty, guard at White Sulphur Springs, Georgia, December 31, 1864. Paroled, Atlanta, Georgia, 1865 ★ Chastain, R. M. -- 2nd Corporal - April 22, 1861. Absent without leave April 15-December 31, 1864 ★ Claiborne, John L. -- Private - April 22, 1861. Elected 2nd Lieutenant September 17, 1862. Killed, Sharpsburg, Maryland September 17, 1862 ★ Cochran, Thomas J. -- Private - April 22, 1861. Died in Richmond, Virginia hospital December 19, 1861 ★ Cole, William M. -- Private - April 22, 1861. Received pay February 17, 1865 ★ Cornett, Andrew C. -- Private - April 22, 1861. Appears last on roll for July 1, 1861 ★ Cornett, Andrew J. -- Private - April 22, 1861. Lost eye and captured, Gettysburg, Pennsylvania July 2, 1863. Paroled at U. S. Hospital, Chester, Pennsylvania 1863. Received, City Point, Virginia for exchange September 23, 1863 ★ Cox, James M. -- Private - August 17, 1861. Admitted to General Hospital with measles October 9, 1861. Discharged, under age, July 18, 1862 ★ Cox, John -- Private - 1861. Admitted to Chimborazo Hospital #1, Richmond, Virginia, October 24, 1861. Transferred to 2nd Georgia Hospital 1861. Admitted to Chimborazo Hospital #3, Richmond, Virginia with debility, November 27, 1861. Transferred to 2nd Georgia Hospital November 28, 1861. No later record ★ Denson, J. M. -- 1st Lieutenant - July 18, 1861. -- See 2nd Sergeant Company G ★ Denton, Jonathan L. -- Private - April 22, 1861. Appointed Corporal. Roll for December 31, 1864, last on file, shows him present ★ Dobbs, Stephen C. -- 1st Sergeant - April 22, 1861. Elected Captain Company E, 11th Regiment, Georgia Infantry, July 3, 1861. Resigned December 1, 1863 ★ Doyle, William Turner -- See 1st Sergeant Company A ★ Ellis, John J. -- Private - April 22, 1861. Appointed Corporal. Deserted September 29, 1864. Received, Washington, D. C., a Confederate deserter, where he took oath of allegiance to U. S. Government and was released October 3, 1864 ★ Florence, Thomas W. -- Private - March 1862. Appointed Sergeant. Severely wounded in hip, Jonesboro, Georgia, August 31, 1864. Admitted to Ocmulgee Hospital, Macon, Georgia September 25, 1864. Died, wounds, October 27, 1864 ★ German, Larkin -- 2nd Lieutenant - April 22, 1861. Appears last on roll for July 1, 1861. No record of transfer or discharge found, but he was appointed 1st Sergeant, Company B, 65th Regiment, Georgia Infantry, July 4, 1862. Elected 2nd Lieutenant January 30, 1864;1st Lieutenant March 1864. Surrendered, Greensboro, North Carolina April 26, 1865 ★ German, Thomas D. -- Private - April 22, 1861. . Surrendered, Appomattox, Virginia April 9, 1865 ★ Goddard, J. T. -- 1st Lieutenant - April 22, 1861. Resigned July 18, 1861 ★ Gosnell, Alfred -- Private - April 22, 1861. Absent without leave April 15-December 31, 1864 ★ Gosnell, George W. -- Private - April 22, 1861. Wounded and captured, Sharpsburg, Maryland September 17, 1862. Died, wounds, Locust Springs Hospital, Fredericksburg, Maryland October 6, 1862 ★ Greene, Richard -- Private - April 22, 1861. Died July 15, 1861 ★ Greer, James A. -- Private - April 22, 1861. Appears last on roll for July 1, 1861 ★ Harris, Lewis -- Private - April 22, 1861. Appears last on roll for July 1, 1861 ★ Havniear, Henry N. -- Private - April 22, 1861. Received pay at Richmond, Virginia July 12, 1862. Discharged 1862. Appears also as Havemier, Havenar and Havinear ★ Hice, Columbus -- Private - April 22, 1861. Appointed 1st Sergeant July 3, 1861. Roll for December 31, 1864, last on file, shows him present. No later record ★ Hicks, Joseph -- Private - April 22, 1861. Appears last on roll for July 1, 1861 ★ Hughes, William -- Private - April 22, 1861. Appears last on roll for July 1, 1861 ★ Jones, James M. -- Private - August 17, 1861. Wounded at Malvern Hill, Virginia July 1, 1862; 2nd Manassas, Virginia August 30, 1862. Surrendered, Appomattox, Virginia April 9, 1865 ★ Jones, John L. -- Private - April 22, 1861. Died in Manassas, Virginia hospital December 17, 1861 ★ Kincaid, Benjamin Franklin -- 2nd Sergeant - April 22, 1861. Elected 2nd Lieutenant April 28, 1862; 1st Lieutenant September 17, 1862. Wounded in left arm and right leg, Sharpsburg, Maryland September 17, 1862. Arm amputated. Resigned, disability, January 9, 1864 ★ Kincaid, Joseph -- Private - April 22, 1861. Discharged at Richmond, Virginia, exempt, being a Minister of the Gospel, July 1862. Born in Haywood County, North Carolina February 22, 1823. Died in Murray County, Georgia February 12, 1912 ★ Kincaid, W. R. -- Private - March 1, 1863. Wounded in left foot and shoulder and captured, Gettysburg, Pennsylvania July 2, 1863. Paroled, DeCamp General Hospital, David's Island, New York and sent to City Point, Virginia for exchange September 27, 1863. Disabled by wounds December 31, 1864 ★ Kincaid, William Jefferson -- Private - April 22, 1861. Appears last on roll for July 1, 1861 ★ Kindall, Benjamin P. -- Private - April 22, 1861. Elected Ensign February 10, 1862; 1st Lieutenant January 9, 1864. Surrendered, Appomattox, Virginia April 9, 1865 ★ Kindall, John N. -- Private - April 22, 1861. Wounded, Malvern Hill, Virginia July 1, 1862; Chickamauga, Georgia September 19, 1863; Petersburg, Virginia July 1864. Surrendered, Appomattox, Virginia April 9, 1865 ★ Kindall, William -- Private - April 22, 1861. Appears last on roll for July 1, 1861 ★ Kinser, William -- Private - April 22, 1861. Died, measles, Brunswick, Georgia June 27, 1861 ★ Kleaber, E. A. -- Private - April 22, 1861. Roll dated August 31, 1864, shows him absent without leave since July 18, 1862. No later record ★ Lewis, William -- Private - April 22, 1861. Roll for December 31, 1864, last on file, shows him on detached duty, nurse in hospital ★ Mathis, W. R. -- Private - August 17, 1861. Roll for December 31, 1864, last on file, shows him absent without leave from March 7, 1864 ★ McCall, Claiborne W. -- Private - April 22, 1861. Appears last on roll for July 1, 1861 ★ McMinn, Jasper N. -- Private - April 22, 1861. Information of death received but not official. Name ordered dropped from rolls October 31, 1862 ★ McMinn, Robert -- Private - April 22, 1861. Killed at Malvern Hill, Virginia July 1, 1862 ★ Moody, Thomas A. -- Private - April 22, 1861. Appears only on roll for July 1, 1861 ★ Moreland, George W. -- Private - April 22, 1861. Appointed Sergeant. Surrendered, Appomattox, Virginia April 9, 1865 ★ Morris, Thomas J. -- Private - April 22, 1861.

Elected Captain April 28, 1862. Roll for December 31, 1864, last on file, shows him present ★ Morris, W. A. -- 4th Sergeant - April 22, 1861. Appears last on roll for July 1, 1861 ★ Mull, Daniel B. -- Private - April 22, 1861. Appears last on roll for July 1, 1861 ★ Murray, R. F. -- Private - August 17, 1861. Wounded, Wilderness, Virginia May 6, 1864. Surrendered, Greensboro, North Carolina April 26, 1865. The 2nd Regiment, Georgia Infantry, was surrendered at Appomattox, Virginia. The above named soldier was one of a number of men absent from their commands at the time of surrender and was consequently paroled at Greensboro, North Carolina, on a later date, as of the 2nd Regiment, Georgia Infantry ★ Murray, William M. -- Private - April 22, 1861. Appears last on roll for July 1, 1861 ★ Odom, John (or Odum) -- Private - August 19, 1862. Took oath of allegiance to U. S. Government, Washington, D. C., March 14, 1864 ★ O'Shields, J. M. -- Private - August 17, 1861. Absent without leave February 24-December 31, 1864 ★ Oxford, E. J. -- Private. Appointed Sergeant. Wounded, Jonesboro, Georgia August 31, 1864. Admitted to 2nd Division Hospital, 15th Army Corps, near Jonesboro, Georgia, where left leg was amputated, September 1, 1864 ★ Parton, Charles M. -- Private - April 22, 1861. Appears last on roll for July 1, 1861 ★ Patterson, J. B. -- Private - April 22, 1861. Died, Savannah, Georgia hospital June 1861 ★ Phillips, Green F. -- Private - April 22, 1861. Wounded, Gettysburg, Pennsylvania July 2, 1863. Surrendered, Appomattox, Virginia April 9, 1865 ★ Porter, David H. -- Private - April 22, 1861. Died, Lynchburg, Virginia October 26, 1862 ★ Porter, Samuel G., Jr. -- Private - April 22, 1861. Died March 20, 1862. Buried Oakland Cemetery, Atlanta, Georgia ★ Powell, Marcus L. -- Private - April 29, 1861. Absent without leave November 7-December 31, 1864 ★

Rice, William E. -- 1st Corporal - April 22, 1861. Appears last on roll for July 1, 1861 ★ Rogers, James R. -- Private - March 25, 1864. Paroled, Augusta, Georgia May 20, 1865 ★ Sanders, Patrick -- Private - August 17, 1861. Deserted August 25, 1863 ★ Shepherd, John S. -- 3rd Corporal - April 22, 1861. Roll for December 31, 1864, last on file, shows him present ★ Smith, Harvey N. -- Private - April 22, 1861. Died June 6, 1862 ★ Sparks, John J. -- Private - April 22, 1861. Appears last on roll for July 1, 1861 ★ Trammell, John B. -- Private - April 22, 1861. Elected 2nd Lieutenant September 17, 1862. Wounded and captured, Gettysburg, Pennsylvania July 2, 1863. Paroled, Fort Delaware, Delaware and forwarded to City Point, Virginia for exchange February 27, 1865 ★ Trammell, Thomas R. -- Private - April 22, 1861. Elected 2nd Lieutenant, Company E, 11th Regiment, Georgia Infantry, July 3, 1861; 1st Lieutenant October 15, 1862; Captain and Assistant Quartermaster, 11th Regiment, Georgia Infantry1864. Surrendered, Appomattox, Virginia April 9, 1865 ★ Turner, William J. -- Private - April 22, 1861. Roll for December 31, 1864, last on file, shows him on detached service ★ Underwood, John E. -- Private - April 22, 1861. Appears last on roll for July 1, 1861 ★ Vestal, Jeremiah -- Private - April 22, 1861. Wounded, Malvern Hill, Virginia July 1, 1862. Died, wounds, Richmond, Virginia hospital November 24, 1862 ★ Wakefield, Thomas J. -- Private - April 22, 1861. Deserted September 29, 1864. Captured September 30, 1864. Received at Defenses South of Potomac, Washington, D. C., where he took oath of allegiance to U. S. Government and was furnished transportation to Cleveland, Ohio, October 3, 1864 ★ Weaver, Newton -- Private - April 22, 1861. Appears last on roll for July 1, 1861.

COMPANY F, 2ND REGIMENT
CHEROKEE COUNTY "CHEROKEE BROWN RIFLEMEN"

Baker, Sim -- Private. Wounded in hand, Lookout Mountain, Tennessee, November 24, 1863. Never returned to company ★ Baker, William G. -- Private - April 18, 1861. Captured near Suffolk, Virginia May 4, 1863. Exchanged, City Point, Virginia May 23, 1863. Killed, Chickamauga, Georgia September 19, 1863 ★ Barton, Joseph B. -- Private - April 18, 1861. Elected 2nd Lieutenant July 3, 1863. Wounded, Darbytown, Virginia October 7, 1864. Captured, Richmond, Virginia hospital April 3, 1865. Released, U. S. General Hospital, Pt. Lookout, Maryland July 17, 1865 ★ Bennett, Samuel Kibrell -- Private - May 23, 1861. Wounded and captured, Gettysburg, Pennsylvania July 3, 1863. Paroled, David's Island, New York September 1863. Exchanged, City Point, Virginia September 8, 1863. Surrendered, Appomattox, Virginia April 9, 1865 ★ Black, Moses W. -- Enlisted as a private in Company K, 14th Regiment, Georgia Infantry, July 9, 1861. Transferred to Company F, 2nd Regiment, Georgia Infantry, in exchange for W. R. Millwood March 7, 1862. Appointed 3rd Corporal 1863. Roll for December 31, 1864, last on file, shows him absent without leave ★ Bragg, Miles F. -- Private - April 18, 1861. Surrendered, Appomattox, Virginia April 9, 1865 ★ Brand, Joseph N. -- Private - April 18, 1861. Discharged, disability, 1861 ★ Broadwell, James M. -- Private - March 7, 1864. Substitute for F. D. Vernon. Captured and paroled, Anderson, South Carolina May 3, 1865 ★ Broadwell, John M. -- Private - June 28, 1863. Substitute for J. R. McKinney. Roll for December 31, 1864, last on file, shows him present ★ Bruce, Calton -- Private - January 28, 1863. Wounded, Cold Harbor, Virginia June 1, 1864. Roll for December 31, 1864, last on file, shows him absent without leave ★ Carpenter, Jasper W. -- Private - April 18, 1861. Died, Richmond, Virginia hospital March or April 1862 ★ Coker, Thomas D. -- Private - April 18, 1861. Wounded. On wounded furlough August 31, 1864. Roll for December 31, 1864, last on file, shows him absent without leave ★ Collum, John -- Private - April 18, 1861. Discharged, over-age ★ Copeland, Daniel -- Private - May 8, 1861. Discharged, disability, January 9, 1862 ★ Couch, John W. -- Private - April 18, 1861. Killed, Petersburg, Virginia July 10, 1864 ★ Daniel, Francis Marion -- Jr. 2nd Lieutenant - April 18, 1861. Retired April 28, 1862. Died 1912 ★ Daniel, Henry G. -- 2nd Sergeant - April 18, 1861. Elected Jr. 2nd Lieutenant April 28, 1862; 2nd Lieutenant August 30, 1862;1st Lieutenant July 3, 1863. Wounded in arm, resulting in amputation, Wilderness, Virginia May 6, 1864. Absent, wounded, close of war ★ Daniel, William -- 3rd Sergeant - April 18, 1861. Discharged, disability, November 12, 1861 ★ Deaton, John D. -- Private - April 18, 1861. Discharged, disability, 1861 ★ Dickerson, Israel C. -- Private - April 18, 1861. Died, Richmond, Virginia hospital May 31, 1862 ★ Dickerson, Nelson L. -- 1st Sergeant - April 18, 1861. Elected 1st Lieutenant April 28, 1862; Captain August 30, 1862. Killed, Gettysburg, Pennsylvania July 3, 1863 ★ Dickerson, Thomas E. -- Captain - April 18, 1861. Retired April 28, 1862 ★ Donaldson, M. G. -- 1st Lieutenant - July 16, 1861. Retired April 28, 1862 ★ Doss, Robert L. -- Private - April 18, 1861. Killed, Gettysburg, Pennsylvania July 2, 1863 ★ Doss, William J. -- Private - April 18, 1861. Appointed 1st Sergeant April 28, 1862. Roll for December 31, 1864, last on file, shows him present ★ Downs, John H. -- Corporal - May 7, 1864. Roll for February 28, 1865, last on file, shows him present ★ Ellison, Richard -- Private - May 23, 1861. Appears last on roll for June 30, 1861 ★ Evans, John G. -- Private - April 18, 1861. Discharged, disability, November 23, 1861. Enlisted as a private, Company B, 43rd Regiment, Georgia Infantry, March 10, 1862. Captured, Vicksburg, Mississippi July 4, 1863, and paroled there July 7, 1863. Wounded and permanently disabled, Jonesboro, Georgia, August 31, 1864. (Born in Georgia April 10, 1844.) ★ Evans, Joseph M. -- Private - April 18, 1861. Appears last on roll for June 30, 1861 ★ Ferguson, Milligan F. -- Private - April 18, 1861. On detached duty December 31, 1864. No later record ★ Finch, Ivy A. -- Private - May 16, 1861. Wounded, Sharpsburg, Maryland

September 17, 1862. Discharged, having been appointed a commissioned officer, August 6, 1864 ★ Finch, Thomas E. -- Private - April 18, 1861. Appears last an roll for June 30, 1861 ★ Fowler, Leonard R. -- Private - April 18, 1861. Killed in railroad accident 1863 ★ Freeman, Henry F. -- Private - April 18, 1861. Wounded, Wilderness, Virginia and sent to General Hospital May 6, 1864. Absent, wounded, December 31, 1864. No later record ★ Garrison, William E. -- Private - April 18, 1861. Killed, Garnett's Farm, Virginia June 27, 1862 ★ Gayden, Andrew -- Private - 1863. Substitute for C. A. Pierce. Captured, Gettysburg, Pennsylvania July 3, 1863. Took oath of allegiance to U. S. Government and enlisted in U. S. service October 1, 1863 ★ Hampton, George W. -- Private - April 18, 1861. Died, Camp Walker near Manassas, Virginia August 9, 1861. Buried Hollywood Cemetery, Richmond, Virginia ★ Harris, Alpheus Skidmore -- 1st Lieutenant - April 18, 1861. Elected Lieutenant Colonel May 14, 1861; Colonel, 43rd Regiment, Georgia Infantry, March 20, 1863. Killed, Baker's Creek, Mississippi May 16, 1863 ★ Harris, James -- Private - April 18, 1861. Appointed 1st Sergeant August 30, 1862. Surrendered, Appomattox, Virginia April 9, 1865 ★ Hatcher, Henry D. -- Private - May 23, 1861. Wounded, Chickamauga, Georgia September 19, 1863. Roll for December 31, 1864, last on file, shows him absent without leave ★ Hawkins, Charles A. -- Musician - April 18, 1861. Transferred to Regimental Band May 15, 1861. Surrendered, Appomattox, Virginia April 9, 1865 ★ Heard, John G. -- 3rd Corporal - April 18, 1861. Elected 2nd Lieutenant April 28, 1862; 1st Lieutenant August 30, 1862; Captain July 3, 1863. Furloughed for 29 days from February 1, 1865. Unable to return to command on account of Sherman's army. Enlisted in Georgia Militia 1865. Surrendered, Kingston, Georgia May 12, 1865. Died, Marietta, Georgia April 4, 1919 ★ Heard, Joseph W. -- Private - April 18, 1861. Appointed Sergeant. Wounded, Chickamauga, Georgia September 19, 1863. Received pay January 2, 1865. No later record ★ Hilhouse, William F. -- Private - April 18, 1861. Roll for December 31, 1864, last on file, shows him absent without leave ★ Hitchens, John -- Private - May 23, 1861. Appears last on roll for June 30, 1861 ★ Holland, Oscar A. -- Private - April 18, 1861. Wounded in railroad accident, Atlanta, Georgia, December 28, 1864. Died, wounds, Empire Hospital, Atlanta, Georgia, January 28, 1864. Buried there in Oakland Cemetery ★ Hood, Humphrey -- Private - December 22, 1862. Wounded, Chickamauga, Georgia September 19, 1863. Died, wounds, November 13, 1863 ★ Howard, Thomas S. -- Private - April 18, 1861. Appointed Corporal. Wounded, Petersburg, Virginia and sent to General Hospital July 21, 1864. Died, wounds, in 1864 ★ Hutson, L. A. (or Hudson) -- Private - May 23, 1861. Died, 3rd Georgia Hospital, Richmond, Virginia March 28, 1862 ★ Ingram, William A. -- Private - April 18, 1861. Died in hospital 1861 ★ Jackson, Jasper -- Private - April 18, 1861. Discharged, over age, in 1862 ★ Jones, John T. -- Private - April 18, 1861. Wounded. Roll for December 31, 1864, last on file, shows him absent without leave ★ Jordon, James L. -- 2nd Corporal - April 18, 1861. Appointed 3rd Sergeant 1861. Discharged, disability, December 28, 1861 ★ Kennett, Z. D. -- Private - May 23, 1861. Died in hospital 1861 ★ King, Adoniron S. -- Private - April 18, 1861. Roll for June 30, 1861, shows him present. No later record in this company. Enlisted as a private, Company B, 43rd Regiment, Georgia Infantry, March 10, 1862. Captured, Baker's Creek, Mississippi May 16, 1863. Exchanged. Appointed 2nd Sergeant February 1864. Took oath of allegiance to U. S. Government, Chattanooga, Tennessee, August 28, 1864. Captured, Cherokee County, Georgia, 1864. Took oath of allegiance to U. S. Government, Louisville, Kentucky, September 26, 1864 ★ Langston, Jesse B. -- 1st Corporal - April 18, 1861. Discharged July 18, 1862 ★ Loveless, Samuel B. -- Private - April 18, 1861. Died, pneumonia, November 16, 1861 ★ Manders, James A. -- Private - April 18, 1861. Appointed Corporal. Surrendered, Appomattox, Virginia April 9, 1865 ★ McCollum, Benjamin Franklin -- Private - April 18, 1861.

Discharged, under-age, 1862 ★ McCollum, John W. -- 4th Sergeant - April 18, 1861. Discharged 1862 ★ McCrary, Andrew J. -- Private - April 18, 1861. Killed, Petersburg, Virginia June 19, 1864 ★ McKinney, J. R. -- Private. Discharged, furnished John M. Broadwell as substitute, June 28, 1863 ★ Millwood, William R. -- Private - May 23, 1861. Transferred to Company K, 14th Regiment, Georgia Infantry, in exchange for Moses W. Black March 7, 1862. Captured near Petersburg, Virginia March 25, 1865. Released, Pt. Lookout, Maryland June 29, 1865 ★ Moore, Edward L. -- Private - April 18, 1861. Died 1861 ★ Moore, W. J. -- Private - July 17, 1861. Roll for October 31, 1861, shows he was sent to Richmond, Virginia sick October 6, 1861. No later record ★ Morgan, Thomas J. -- Private - May 23, 1861. Discharged prior to March 26, 1862 ★ Morgan, William N. -- Private - May 23, 1861. Died, disease, March 4, 1862 ★ Moss, William G. -- Private - April 18, 1861. Discharged, disability, 1861 ★ Mullins, Henry L. -- Private - April 18, 1861. Died August 12, 1862 ★ Mullins, John T. -- Private - April 18, 1861. Died, disease, Cherokee County, Georgia May 23, 1863 ★ Nix, John -- Private - April 18, 1861. Wounded. Roll for December 31, 1864, last on file, shows him absent without leave ★ Nix, William -- 4th Corporal - April 18, 1861. Wounded, Yorktown, Virginia April 5, 1862. Discharged, disability, July 11, 1862 ★ Owens, Thomas C. -- Musician - April 18, 1861. Wounded, Gaines Mills, Virginia June 27, 1862. Died, Richmond, Virginia hospital July 1, 1862 ★ Padget, Irvin (or Ervin) -- Private - April 18, 1861. Took oath of allegiance to U. S. Government, Chattanooga, Tennessee, and released March 14, 1864 ★ Pierce, Clemeth A. -- Private - April 18, 1861. Discharged, furnished Andrew Gayden as substitute, 1863 ★ Pierce, George W. -- Private - April 18, 1861. Transferred to Regimental Band May 15, 1861. Wounded, Garnett's Farm, Virginia June 27, 1862 ★ Pinson, Thomas J. -- Private - April 18, 1861. Captured 1864. Deserted August 24, 1864 ★ Putnam, Berry P. -- Private - April 18, 1861. Appointed Regimental Musician May 15, 1861. Surrendered, Appomattox, Virginia April 9, 1865 ★ Ragsdale, Allen B. -- Private - April 18, 1861. Discharged 1861 ★ Reinhart, Augustus M. (or Rheinhart) -- Private - April 18, 1861. Discharged, disability, Richmond, Virginia January 6, 1862. Elected 1st Lieutenant, Company A, 43rd Regiment, Georgia Infantry, March 10, 1862; Captain July 15, 1862. Wounded, Baker's Creek, Mississippi May 16, 1863. Resigned January 8, 1864. (Born June 21, 1842.) ★ Rice, Joseph -- Private - April 18, 1861. Roll for December 31, 1864, last on file, shows him absent without leave ★ Rice, William -- Private - April 18, 1861. Discharged, over-age, 1862

★ Richardson, Jasper A. -- Private - April 18, 1861. Surrendered, Appomattox, Virginia April 9, 1865. Died, Murray County, Georgia July 5, 1927 ★ Richardson, Nathan -- Private - April 18, 1861. Captured, Gettysburg, Pennsylvania July 3, 1863. Took oath of allegiance to U. S. Government, Pt. Lookout, Maryland, and enlisted in U. S. service January 24, 1864 ★ Robertson, Nathaniel -- Private - May 23, 1861. Captured, Gettysburg, Pennsylvania July 3, 1863. Received, Venus Point, Savannah River, Georgia for exchange November 15, 1864. No later record ★ Seay, Dorsey H. -- Private - April 20, 1861. Died April 27, 1862. Buried Hollywood Cemetery, Richmond, Virginia ★ Shuford, Alonzo B. -- 2nd Lieutenant - April 18, 1861. Elected Captain April 28, 1862. Killed, 2nd Manassas, Virginia August 30, 1862 ★ Smallwood, Allen G. -- Private - April 18, 1861. Appears last on roll for June 30, 1861 ★ Smith, Lewis T. -- Private - August 7, 1862. Roll for December 31, 1864, last on file, shows he was transferred to Company B. No later record ★ Staner, Michael -- Private - April 18, 1861. Killed, Garnett's Farm, Virginia June 27, 1862 ★ Starr, John T. -- Private. Wounded in arm, resulting in amputation, July 4, 1864. Captured (gave himself up), Monocracy, Maryland, September 22, 1864. Released, Fort McHenry, Maryland and sent to Headquarters, Middle Department October 22, 1864 ★ Strickland, Joseph G. -- Private - April 18, 1861. - Appears last on roll for June 30, 1861 ★ Thomas, Waddie -- Private. Substitute. Killed, Chickamauga, Georgia September 19, 1863 ★ Tidwell, Francis M. -- Private - April 18, 1861. Appears last on roll for June 30, 1861 ★ Tierce, William F. -- Private - April 18, 1861. Discharged, over-age ★ Turner, McCager (or McAger) -- Private - January 28, 1863. Captured, Chickamauga, Georgia September 19, 1863. Released, Camp Douglas, Illinois June 20, 1865 ★ Vernon, Franklin D. -- Private - April 20, 1861. Discharged, furnished James M. Broadwell as substitute, March 7, 1864 ★ Watson, Alfred H. -- Private - April 18, 1861. Wounded, Garnett's Farm, Virginia June 27, 1862. Died, wounds, Richmond, Virginia July 9, 1862 ★ Watson, Joseph G. -- Private - April 18, 1861. Discharged, having been appointed a commissioned officer in Georgia State Troops, December 22, 1862 ★ Wheeler, James A. -- Private - April 18, 1861. Appears last on roll for June 30, 1861 ★ Wheeler, James W. -- Private. Took oath of allegiance to U. S. Government, Chattanooga, Tennessee, May 5, 1864 ★ Wheeler, William P. -- Private - April 18, 1861. Severely wounded in back of neck, Wilderness, Virginia May 6, 1864. Home, wounded furlough, close of war. Born in Georgia. Died, Forsyth County, Georgia, May 10, 1935 ★ Williams, F. P. -- Private - April 18, 1861. Appears last on roll for June 30, 1861.

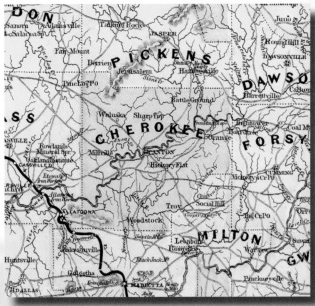

COMPANY G, 2ND REGIMENT
MUSCOGEE "COLUMBUS GUARDS"

Abercrombie, George H. -- Private - April 16, 1861. Transferred to Company G, 7th Regiment Alabama Cavalry March 13, 1863. Elected 2nd Lieutenant July 22, 1863. Roll for December 31, 1863, last on file, shows him present ★ Abercrombie, Wiley -- Private - April 16, 1861. Transferred to Company G, 7th Regiment Alabama Cavalry August 27, 1863. Appointed 1st Lieutenant and A. D. C. to Major General S. D. French August 11, 1864. No later record ★ Acee, A. E. -- Private - April 16, 1861. Discharged, disability, October 26, 1861 ★ Acee, O. S. -- Private - April 16, 1861. Absent, sick, Richmond, Virginia hospital October 31, 1861. No later record ★ Allen, John S., Jr. -- 1st Sergeant - April 16, 1861. Appointed 1st Lieutenant and Adjutant, 43rd Regiment, Georgia Infantry, September 26, 1862, to rank from May 15, 1862. Captured, Vicksburg, Mississippi July 4, 1863 and paroled there July 6, 1863. Roll dated December 31, 1863, last on file, shows him present ★ Anderson, W. L. -- Private - April 16, 1861. Appointed Corporal. Surrendered, Appomattox, Virginia April 9, 1865 ★ Andrews, S. R. Jr. -- Private - April 16, 1861. Appears last on roll for October 31, 1861. Transferred to Artillery ★ Apple, Alfred -- Musician - April 16, 1861. Transferred to Regimental Band May 15, 1861. Detailed with Company F, 19th Battalion, Georgia State Guards August 3, 1863. Roll dated December 31, 1864, last on file, shows him on detail in Ordnance Department, Columbus, Georgia. No later record ★ Bacon, Robert A. -- Private - April 16, 1861. Discharged, disability, November 8, 1861 ★ Bailey, C. A. -- Private - April 16, 1861. Killed, Gettysburg, Pennsylvania July 2, 1863 ★ Ballard, John J. -- Private - February 1, 1864. Died, Winder Hospital, Richmond, Virginia July 15, 1864 ★ Banks, E. -- Private - April 16, 1861. Elected 2nd Lieutenant, Company F, 39th Regiment Alabama Infantry June 9, 1863. Killed, Resaca, Georgia, May 14, 1864 ★ Banks, W. -- Private - April 16, 1861. Killed, Atlanta, Georgia July 22, 1864 ★ Barden, William Alfred -- Private - April 16, 1861. Elected 2nd Lieutenant of Company H, 17th Regiment, Georgia Infantry, August 15, 1861; 1st Lieutenant November 1, 1861; Captain June 2, 1862; Major January 22, 1864; Lieutenant Colonel September 22, 1864, to rank from January 22, 1864. At Danville, Virginia close of war ★ Barnard, T. M. -- Private - April 16, 1861. Absent without leave October 31, 1861. No later record ★ Beasley, T. M. -- Private - April 16, 1861. Elected Lieutenant 1861. Appears last on roll for October 31, 1861 ★ Bedell, J. R. -- Private - April 16, 1861. Appears last on roll for October 31, 1861 ★ Bedell, William R. -- Private - April 16, 1861. Elected 2nd Lieutenant, Company C. 46th Regiment, Georgia Infantry, March 4, 1862. Appointed Adjutant June 17, 1863. Elected 1st Lieutenant, Company C. Surrendered, Greensboro, North Carolina April 28, 1865 ★ Beecher, H. B. -- Private - April 16, 1861. Appointed Sergeant Major April 16, 1862. Sick in General Hospital June 10-December 31, 1864. No later record ★ Bethune, J. G. -- Private - April 16, 1861. Appears last on roll for October 31, 1861 ★ Bethune, Joseph D. -- Private - July 25, 1861. Sick in General Hospital December 31, 1864. No later record ★ Blalock, J. D. -- Private - April 26, 1864. Surrendered, Appomattox, Virginia April 9, 1865 ★ Blanchard, Thomas E. -- Private - April 16, 1861. Elected Jr. 2nd Lieutenant Company F, 3rd Battalion, Georgia Infantry July 12, 1861; 2nd Lieutenant October 31, 1861; Captain Company B, 37th Regiment, Georgia Infantry, May 6, 1863. Detailed Acting Adjutant General on Staff of General W. B. Bates December 31, 1862 to May 1864. Wounded and permanently disabled, Resaca, Georgia May 14, 1864. Served as Adjutant of Post at Columbus, Georgia, 1864 to close of war ★ Booher, D. B. (or Brosnichee) -- Private - April 16, 1861. Elected Lieutenant 1864. Killed, Crater near Petersburg, Virginia July 30, 1864. Buried Stonewall Cemetery, LaGrange, Georgia ★ Briggs, Edmund B. -- Private - April 16, 1861. Appointed Quartermaster Sergeant April 16, 1861; 1st Lieutenant and A. D. C., and ordered to report to General P. J. Semmes July 10, 1862, to rank form April 10, 1862. Resigned May 25, 1863 ★ Brosnichee, D. B. -- See Booher, D. B ★ Brown, William A. -- Private - April 16, 1861. Transferred to Nelson's Independent Company Georgia Cavalry, June 20, 1862. Roll for August 31, 1863, last on file, shows him sick since August 15th. No later record ★ Burch, J. F. -- Private - April 16, 1861. Appointed Hospital Steward October 3, 1862. Elected Lieutenant. Killed, Petersburg, Virginia June 15, 1864

★ Butt, W. B. -- Private - April 16, 1861. Sick, Richmond, Virginia August 15-October 31, 1861. No later record ★ Calhoun, A. A. -- Private - April 16, 1861. Appears last on roll for October 31, 1861 ★ Calhoun, J. C. -- Private - April 16, 1861. Appointed Captain and Assistant Quartermaster. No later record ★ Carter, John D. Jr. -- Private - April 16, 1861. Appointed Corporal. Wounded 1861. Paid for commutation of rations March 24, 1863, for period December 1, 1861 to May 31, 1862, while absent, wounded ★ Carter, T. M. -- Private - April 16, 1861. Transferred to Nelson's Independent Company Georgia Cavalry, June 20, 1862. Surrendered, Greensboro, North Carolina April 26, 1865. Born in Georgia 1841 ★ Chaffin, Thomas Jr. -- 4th Corporal - April 16, 1861. Appointed Sergeant. Elected Captain November 17, 1864. Commanding regiment at surrender, Appomattox, Virginia April 9, 1865 ★ Clapp, J. J. -- Private - April 16, 1861. Appears last on roll for October 31, 1861 ★ Clemens, Welcom G. -- 2nd Lieutenant - April 16, 1861. Appointed Major and Assistant Quartermaster of Cumming's Brigade October 29, 1862. No later record ★ Cody, J. Adolphus -- Private - April 16, 1861. Wounded in leg, resulting in amputation, Missionary Ridge, Tennessee November 25, 1863. Appointed Captain and A. A. I. G., Cumming's Brigade, November 1863 ★ Coleman, A. A. -- Private - April 16, 1861. Discharged by order Secretary of War. August 8, 1861 ★ Coleman, C. -- Private - April 16, 1861. Wounded and disabled, date and place not stated. On detail duty in Quartermaster Department, account of wounds, December 31, 1864 ★ Coleman, T. G. -- Private - April 16, 1861. Appointed 4th Sergeant May 15, 1862. Wounded, Wilderness, Virginia May 6, 1864. Surrendered, Appomattox, Virginia April 9, 1865 ★ Croft, William G. -- Private - April 16, 1861. Elected Jr. 2nd Lieutenant, Croft's Battery, Georgia Light Artillery, November 27, 1861. Roll for August 31, 1864, last on file, shows him present. Born Columbus, Georgia April 9, 1838 ★ Cromwell, Oliver -- Private - April 16, 1861. Wounded and captured, date and place not stated. Exchanged September 27, 1863. On detail duty in Commissary Department, account of wounds, December 31, 1864 ★ Crowell, John H. -- Private - July 25, 1861. Transferred to Nelson's Independent Company Georgia Cavalry, June 20, 1862. Surrendered, Greensboro, North Carolina April 26, 1865 ★ Daniel, Robert A. -- Private - April 16, 1861. Surrendered, Macon, Georgia May 5, 1865 ★ Davis, A. B. -- Private - April 16, 1861. Absent, sick, Manchester, Virginia October 31, 1861. No later record ★ Davis, W. S. -- Private - April 16, 1861. Killed, Cold Harbor, Virginia May 27, 1864 ★ Dawson, D. T. -- Private - April 16, 1861. On detail duty in Quartermaster Department, Columbus, Georgia, December 31, 1864 ★ Denson, J. M. -- 2nd Sergeant - April 16, 1861. Transferred to Company E, and elected 1st Lieutenant July 18, 1861. No later record ★ Devotie, J. G. -- Private - April 16, 1861. Discharged, disability, prior to August 10, 1862 ★ Dillingham, George W. -- Private - April 16, 1861. Appointed Captain and Assistant Commissary October 18, 1861. On duty as Assistant Commissary, 1st Army Corps, Army of Virginia, March 30, 1865. Surrendered, Appomattox, Virginia April 9, 1865 ★ Dixon, H. B. -- Private - July 15, 1861. Died, Richmond, Virginia September 23, 1861 ★ Dixon, S. M. -- Private - April 16, 1861. Sick, Richmond, Virginia September 25-October 31, 1861. No later record ★ Dubose, James C. -- Appointed 3rd Sergeant December 12, 1861. Surrendered, Appomattox, Virginia April 9, 1865 ★ Ellis, Roswell -- Captain - April 16, 1861. Appointed Captain and A. A. General December 28, 1864, to rank from November 17, 1864. Retired March 25, 1865 ★ Etter, Martin -- Private - February 15, 1863. Surrendered, Appomattox, Virginia April 9, 1865 ★ Everett, James M. -- Jr. 2nd Lieutenant April 16, 1861. Retired April 28, 1862. Died, Columbus, Georgia 1863 ★ Fogle, J. A. -- Private - April 16, 1861. Appointed Hospital Steward October 6, 1862; Assistant Surgeon January 21, 1865, to rank from November 14, 1864 ★ Fogle, T. T. -- Private - April 16, 1861. Elected 1st Lieutenant 1864. Killed, Wilderness, Virginia May 6, 1864 ★ Furgeson, W. F. (or Ferguson) -- Private - April 16, 1861. Appears last on roll for October 31, 1861 ★ Girdner, J. L. -- Private - April 16, 1861. Transferred to Regimental Band August 31, 1861. Enlisted as a private in Captain F. M. Brooks' Company, 5th Regiment, Georgia State Guards Infantry August 4, 1863. No later record ★ Hall, H. H. --

Private - July 25, 1861. On temporary detail with Captain Phillips December 31, 1864. No later record ★ Hall, William F. -- Private - April 16, 1861. Surrendered, Appomattox, Virginia April 9, 1865 ★ Harris, A. -- Private - April 16, 1861. Wounded, Darbytown, Virginia October 7, 1864. On wounded furlough December 31, 1864. No later record ★ Hawks, William N. Jr. -- Private - April 16, 1861. Transferred to Nelson's Independent Company Georgia Cavalry, June 20, 1862. Received pay September 15, 1864. No later record ★ Henry, D. C. -- Private - April 16, 1861. Died 1863 ★ Henry, Robert -- Private - April 18, 1862. Captured, Gettysburg, Pennsylvania July 2, 1863. Released, Fort Delaware, Delaware June 16, 1865 ★ Hicks, J. H. -- Private - April 16, 1861. Surrendered, Appomattox, Virginia April 9, 1865 ★ Hodges, J. W. -- Private - April 16, 1861. Appears last an roll for October 31, 1861 ★ Hodges, Wesley C. -- 1st Lieutenant - April 16, 1861. Elected Lieutenant Colonel, 17th Regiment, Georgia Infantry, August 9, 1861; Colonel January 4, 1863. Wounded, Wilderness, Virginia May 6, 1864. On wounded furlough close of war ★ Hogan, J. C. -- Private - April 16, 1861. Roll for December 31, 1864, last on file, shows him absent without leave ★ Holt, Bolling Hall -- Private - April 16, 1861. Discharged October 14, 1861. Elected Major, 35th Regiment, Georgia Infantry, October 14, 1861; Lieutenant Colonel June 1, 1862; Colonel November 1, 1862. Surrendered, Appomattox, Virginia April 9, 1865 ★ Houghton, William R. -- Private - April 16, 1861. Appointed 1st Sergeant July 1, 1862. Received pay January 20, 1865. No later record ★ Howard, J. T. -- Private - April 16, 1861. Discharged, disability, February 18, 1862 ★ Howard, Robert M. -- Private - October 1, 1861. Transferred to Nelson's Independent Company Georgia Cavalry, June 20, 1862. Applied for authority to raise a company of colored troops April 1, 1865 ★ Howard, Robert Newton -- Private - April 16, 1861. Elected 1st Lieutenant Company C, July 24, 1861; Captain 1862. Surrendered, Appomattox, Virginia April 9, 1865 ★ Hudson, Benjamin H. -- Private - April 16, 1861. Elected 2nd Lieutenant Company M, 1st Regiment, Georgia Regulars, September 2, 1861; 1st Lieutenant Company C, August 30, 1862. Roll for June 30, 1864, last on file, shows him present. No later record ★ Johnson, Harris R. -- Appointed 1st Corporal Company C, 9th Regiment, Louisiana Infantry, July 7, 1861. Transferred to Company G, 2nd Regiment, Georgia Infantry, September 26, 1861. Wounded and captured, Wilderness, Virginia May 6, 1864. No later record ★ Johnson, John T. -- Private - April 16, 1861. Discharged October 5, 1861. Re-enlisted. Elected 1st Lieutenant October 15, 1861. Killed, Wilderness, Virginia May 6, 1864 ★ Johnson, L. Q. -- Private - April 16, 1861. Appointed 1st Sergeant July 1, 1862. Elected 1st Lieutenant, Company E, 27th Battalion, Georgia Infantry (Non-conscripts), December 18, 1863. No later record ★ Jones, Boykin -- Private - April 16, 1861. Absent, sick, Richmond, Virginia October 16, 1861. No later record. Born February 15, 1840 ★ Jones, Samuel L. -- Private. Transferred to C. S. Navy and appointed Midshipman 1862. Served on C. S. S. Selma, Mobile, Alabama Fleet, in 1862. No later record ★ Jones, W. E. Jr. -- Private - April 16, 1861. Appointed Sergeant May 1861. Appears last on roll for October 31, 1861, with remark; "Absent, sick, Richmond, Virginia October 6th" ★ Jones, William -- Private - April 16, 1861. Appointed Sergeant Major 1861. Appears last on roll dated October 31, 1861 ★ King, John Edward – Musician - April 16, 1861. Transferred to Regimental Band August 31, 1861. No later record ★ Kyle, W. D. -- Private - April 16, 1861. Received pay May 30, 1862. No later record ★ Lindsay, J. L. (or J. B.) -- Private - April 16, 1861. Paid for rations for 170 days while on sick furlough March 15, 1863. No later record ★ Luckie, C. B. -- Private - April 16, 1861. Appears last on roll for October 31, 1861 ★ Luckie, E. M. -- Private - April 16, 1861. Discharged, disability, October 12, 1861 ★ Marcus, Van -- 3rd Sergeant - April 16, 1861. Appointed Sergeant Major. 15th Regiment Alabama Infantry May 24, 1861. Retired April 13, 1862 ★ Martiniere, William A. -- Private - April 16, 1861. Transferred to Nelson's Independent Company Georgia Cavalry, June 20, 1862. Surrendered, Greensboro, North Carolina April 26, 1865 ★ Mathews, Allen -- Private. Paroled, Montgomery, Alabama June 6, 1865 ★ Mays, G. W. -- Private - April 16, 1861. Appointed Corporal. Elected 2nd Lieutenant; 1st Lieutenant. Killed, Gettysburg, Pennsylvania July 2, 1863 ★ Moses, Montefiore J. -- Private - April 16, 1861. Appointed Assistant Surgeon, 37th Regiment Mississippi Infantry June 2, 1862, to rank from February 17, 1862. Roll for August 31, 1864, last on file, shows him present ★ Moses, W. M. -- Private - April 16, 1861. Roll for December 31, 1864, last on file, shows him sick in General Hospital, Columbus, Georgia ★ Munn, J. R. -- Private - April 16, 1861. Died, Riggie House, Old Braddock, Virginia October 4, 1861 ★ Muse, Thomas H. -- Private - April 16, 1861. Killed, Gettysburg, Pennsylvania July 2, 1863 ★ Owen, David T. (or Owens) -- Private - February 1863. Died, disease, July 1863 ★ Owen, John S. (or Owens) -- Private - April 16, 1861. Transferred to Nelson's Independent Company Georgia Cavalry, and appointed Sergeant June 20, 1862. Elected Jr. 2nd Lieutenant. Surrendered, Greensboro, North Carolina April 26, 1865 ★ Park, T. J. (or J. T.) -- Private - April 16, 1861. Appears last on roll for October 31, 1861 ★

Patterson, W. T. -- Private - April 16, 1861. Elected 2nd Lieutenant July 2, 1863. Killed, Chickamauga, Georgia September 19, 1863 ★ Payne, John O. -- Private - February 20, 1863. Surrendered, Appomattox, Virginia April 9, 1865 ★ Peabody, G. A. -- Private - April 16, 1861. Discharged, disability, December 21, 1861 ★ Perrine, W. H. -- 2nd Corporal - April 16, 1861. Appointed 2nd Sergeant July 18, 1861. On detail duty in Naval Department at Columbus, Georgia January 26-December 31, 1864. No later record ★ Perry, J. C. -- Private - April 16, 1861. Died, Centreville, Virginia October 6, 1861 ★ Pitts, Samuel R. -- Private - April 16, 1861. Appointed 1st Sergeant Company C, August 3, 1861. Elected 2nd Lieutenant April 28, 1862. Wounded, Wilderness, Virginia May 6, 1864. Surrendered, Appomattox, Virginia April 9, 1865 ★ Pope, R. F. (or R. C.) -- Private - August 14, 1861. Paroled, Augusta, Georgia May 18, 1865 ★ Potter, Richard -- 4th Sergeant - April 16, 1861. Appointed 1st Sergeant May 15, 1862. Killed, Malvern Hill, Virginia July 1, 1862 ★ Ragland, Albert E. -- Private - April 16, 1861. Appears last on roll for October 31, 1861. Enlisted as a private, Nelson's Independent Company Georgia Cavalry, June 20, 1862. Roll dated December 1862, last on which borne, shows he was on sick furlough ★ Ragland, George G. -- Private - April 16, 1861. Transferred to Nelson's Independent Company Georgia Cavalry, and elected 1st Lieutenant April 18, 1862; Captain June 27, 1864. Surrendered, Greensboro, North Carolina April 26, 1865 ★ Ragland, O. S. -- 3rd Corporal - April 16, 1861. Appointed 3rd Sergeant May 24, 1861. Discharged, disability, December 12, 1861 ★ Redd, J. K. -- Private - April 16, 1861. Appears last on roll far October 31, 1861. Appointed Aide-de-Camp to General Semmes ★ Redd, N. L. -- Private - April 16, 1861. Discharged, disability, October 14, 1861. Re-enlisted. Elected-Lieutenant ★ Redd, William Jr. -- Private - April 16, 1861. Appointed Color Sergeant 1861. Elected Jr. 2nd Lieutenant Company C, July 24, 1861; 2nd Lieutenant 1862; 1st Lieutenant May 12, 1862. Appointed Regimental Adjutant (to rank from June 14, 1864), December 5, 1864 ★ Ridenhour, Thomas Franklin -- Private - April 16, 1861. Absent, sick, Manchester, Virginia August 10-October 31, 1861. No later record ★ Rntherford, A. H. -- Private - April 16, 1861. Appears last on roll for October 31, 1861 ★ Roberts, N. B. -- Private - April 16, 1861. Discharged, disability, November 7, 1861 ★ Rucker, G. G. -- Private - April 16, 1861. Surrendered, Appomattox, Virginia April 9, 1865 ★ Rucker, Z. G. -- Private - April 16, 1861. Wounded, date and place not stated. On wounded furlough December 31, 1864. No later record ★ Russell, Charles R. -- Private - April 16, 1861. Elected 2nd Lieutenant Company C, July 24, 1861; 1st Lieutenant April 28, 1862. Resigned May 1862. Elected Captain, Company H, 54th Regiment, Georgia Infantry, May 12, 1862. Surrendered, Greensboro, North Carolina April 26, 1865 ★ Rutherford, Robert M. -- Private - April 16, 1861. Transferred to Nelson's Independent Company Georgia Cavalry, June 20, 1862. Captured, Mechanicsburg, Mississippi June 4, 1863. Paroled, Fort Delaware, Delaware February 1865. Received, Boulware & Cox's Wharves, James River, Virginia for exchange March 10-12, 1865 ★ Sanders, J. Henry -- Private - April 16, 1861. Transferred to Regimental Band August 31, 1861. Surrendered, Appomattox, Virginia April 9, 1865 ★ Sanders, J. R. -- 1st Corporal - April 16, 1861. Appointed Sergeant 1861. Appears last on roll for October 31, 1861 ★ Scheussler, L. G. -- Private - April 16, 1861. Appears last on roll for October 31, 1861 ★ Shepherd, William S. -- Private - April 16, 1861. Elected Captain Company C, July 24, 1861; Major September 17, 1862; Lieutenant Colonel July 2, 1863. Wounded, Fort Harrison, Virginia September 29, 1864. At Columbus, Georgia, wounded, January 1, 1865. At Danville, Virginia en route to command when war closed ★ Shorter, Eli S. -- Private - April 16, 1861. Transferred to Company H, 17th Regiment, Georgia Infantry, November 1, 1861. Appointed Quartermaster Sergeant 1862. Surrendered, Appomattox, Virginia April 9, 1865 ★ Slade, J. H. -- Private - April 16, 1861. Wounded and captured, Sharpsburg, Maryland September 17, 1862. Died, wounds, David Smith's Farm, near Sharpsburg, Maryland 1862 ★ Spivey, J. C. -- Private - April 16, 1861. Killed, Sharpsburg, Maryland September 17, 1862 ★ Stewart, Eugene G. -- Private - July 25, 1861. Elected Jr. 2nd Lieutenant December 19, 1864;1st Lieutenant December 19, 1864. Surrendered, Appomattox, Virginia April 9, 1865 ★ Tucker, James Madison -- Private. Took oath of allegiance to U. S. Government at Chattanooga, Tennessee February 20, 1864 ★ Weems, J. A. -- See private Company C ★ Williams, Mitchell A. -- Private - April 16, 1861. Transferred to Nelson's Independent Company Georgia Cavalry, June 20, 1862. Surrendered, Greensboro, North Carolina April 26, 1865 ★ Wise, John -- Private - April 16, 1861. Discharged, disability, August 14, 1861 ★Wooten, M. C. -- Private - April 16, 1861. Appears last on roll for October 31, 1861 ★ Yonge, W. A. -- Private - April 16, 1861. Appears last on roll for October 31, 1861.

98

COMPANY H, 2ND REGIMENT
WHITFIELD COUNTY "WRIGHT INFANTRY"

Ables, Obediah A. -- Private - April 20, 1861. Appointed 3rd Sergeant, April 28, 1862. Killed, Gettysburg, Pennsylvania July 2, 1863 ★Acry, Newton N. -- Private - April 20, 1861. Captured, Chattanooga, Tennessee October 29, 1863. Transferred for exchange February 26, 1865 ★ Ault, John T. -- 1st Lieutenant - April 20, 1861. Retired April 28, 1862. Appointed Adjutant 36th Regiment, Georgia Infantry, November 26, 1862. Declined appointment ★ Bangus, John C. -- 2nd Corporal - April 20, 1861. On detail duty, Quartermaster Department Atlanta, Georgia, October 15, 1863-December 31, 1864 ★ Bates, John -- Private - April 20, 1861. Wounded and captured, Gettysburg, Pennsylvania July 2, 1863. Paroled, DeCamp General Hospital, David's Island, New York in 1863. Received, City Point, Virginia for exchange September 16, 1863. Took oath of allegiance to U. S. Government and sent north of Ohio River February 15, 1865 ★ Beavers, C. B. -- Private - April 20, 1861. On detail duty in Richmond, Virginia hospital August 1, 1861-December 31, 1864 ★ Bennett, John W. -- Private - 1861. Paroled, Augusta, Georgia May 30, 1865 ★ Black, R. M. -- Private - April 20, 1861. Appears last on roll for August 31, 1861 ★ Brewer, E. -- Private - April 20, 1861. Died, typhoid fever, General Hospital #1, Staunton, Virginia, August 19, 1863. Buried there in Thornrose Cemetery ★ Brock, John J. -- Private - April 20, 1861. Discharged, disability, September 12, 1861 ★ Brock, Van Buren -- Private - April 20, 1861. In hospital December 31, 1864. No later record ★ Bruce, George W. -- Jr. 2nd Lieutenant - July 11, 1861. Resigned January 16, 1862 ★ Chandler, John C. -- Private - April 20, 1861. Appointed Sergeant. Killed, Malvern Hill, Virginia July 2, 1862 ★ Chapman, E. E. -- Private - April 22, 1864. Surrendered, Appomattox, Virginia April 9, 1865 ★ Clark, B. B. -- Private - July 1, 1861. Appears last on roll for August 31, 1861 ★ Clark, John J. -- Private - July 1, 1861. Surrendered, Appomattox, Virginia April 9, 1865 ★ Collum, John Basil -- 3rd Sergeant - April 20, 1861. Elected 2nd Lieutenant April 28, 1862; 1st Lieutenant July 2, 1863; Captain June 1, 1864. Surrendered, Appomattox, Virginia April 9, 1865 ★ Cox, F. M. -- Private - April 20, 1861. Died, Whitfield County, Georgia August 6, 1861 ★ Creamer, Garrison -- Private - April 20, 1861. Appears last on roll for August 31, 1861 ★ Creekmore, J. C. -- Private - April 20, 1861. Appears last on roll for August 31, 1861 ★ Crow, W. (or Crew) -- Private - February 3, 1863. Surrendered, Appomattox, Virginia April 9, 1865 ★ Davis, Samuel C. -- Private - April 20, 1861. Appears last on roll for August 31, 1861 ★ Dedmon, John J. -- Private - July 1, 1861. Appears last on roll for August 31, 1861 ★ Dedmon, T. H. -- Private - July 1, 1861. Enlisted for nine months and thirteen days. No later record ★ Dedmon, W. R. -- Private - April 20, 1861. Wounded, Gettysburg, Pennsylvania July 2, 1863. Roll for December 31, 1864, last on file, shows him absent, wounded ★ Dempsey, J. M. -- Private - April 20, 1861. Appears last on roll for August 31, 1861 ★ Dodd, Andrew J. -- Private - April 20, 1861. Appears last on roll for August 31, 1864 ★ Doonan, John J. -- Private - January 6, 1863. Appointed Sergeant; 1st Sergeant. Surrendered, Appomattox, Virginia April 9, 1865 ★ Dycus, Larkin -- Private - April 20, 1861. Appears last on roll for August 31, 1861 ★ Dycus, T. L. -- Private - April 20, 1861. Elected 2nd Lieutenant July 16, 1861. Resigned December 15, 1862 ★ Edwards, Benjamin C. -- Private - April 20, 1861. Appointed 3rd Sergeant May 5, 1864. Surrendered, Appomattox, Virginia April 9, 1865 ★ Edwards, E. H. -- 2nd Lieutenant - April 20, 1861. Resigned July 16, 1861 ★ England, O. M. -- Private - April 20, 1861. Surrendered, Appomattox, Virginia April 9, 1865 ★ Fincher, William Oliver -- Private - April 20, 1861. Discharged, over-age, in 1862. Enlisted as a private; Company A, 4th Regiment, Georgia Cavalry, (Avery's), September 20, 1862. Captured near Knoxville, Tennessee December 3, 1863. Enlisted in U. S. Navy, Rock Island, Illinois and transferred to Naval Rendezvous, Camp Douglas, Illinois January 25, 1864 ★ Glass, W. H. -- Private - April 20, 1861. Died, typhoid pneumonia, near Centerville, Virginia December 24, 1861 ★ Glenn, Jesse A. – Captain - April 20, 1861. Elected Colonel, 36th Regiment, Georgia Infantry, April 24, or July 12, 1862. Captured, Vicksburg, Mississippi July 4, 1863, and paroled there July 9, 1863. Dismissed from service by sentence of Court Martial January 23, 1864 ★ Glenn,

Joseph -- Private - April 20, 1861. Elected Captain, Company A, 36th Regiment, Georgia Infantry, January 15, 1862. Captured, Vicksburg, Mississippi July 4, 1863, and paroled there July 15, 1863. Roll for August 31, 1863, last on file, shows him present ★ Hancock, Benjamin L. -- 2nd Sergeant - April 20, 1861. Elected Captain April 28, 1862. Killed, Gettysburg, Pennsylvania July 2, 1863 ★ Hancock, O. M. -- Private - April 20, 1861. Captured, Williamsport, Maryland September 15, 1862. Exchanged, Aiken's Landing, Virginia November 10, 1862. No later record ★ Hancock, T. B. C. -- Private - April 20, 1861. Elected 1st Lieutenant December 13, 1864. Surrendered, Appomattox, Virginia April 9, 1865 ★ Head, J. M. -- Private - April 20, 1861. Appears last on roll for August 31, 1861 ★ Hendon, L. M. -- Private - January 6, 1863. Wounded, Chickamauga, Georgia September 19, 1863. Captured December 22, 1863. Released June 20, 1865 ★ Higgins, A. M. (or A. N.) -- Private - January 6, 1863. Received, Department of Virginia and North Carolina, a Confederate deserter, March 13, 1865. Took oath of allegiance to U. S. Government and released at Bermuda Hundred, Virginia March 14, 1865 ★ Hobbs, D. T. -- Private - January 6, 1863. Surrendered, Appomattox, Virginia April 9, 1865 ★ Holden, James J. -- Private - July 1, 1861. Discharged, disability, November 2, 1861. Appointed 2nd Sergeant, Company B, 36th Regiment, Georgia Infantry, February 1, 1862. Reduced to 3rd Sergeant May 1, 1863. Captured, Vicksburg, Mississippi July 4, 1863, and paroled there July 9, 1863. Appointed Ensign, 36th Regiment, Georgia Infantry, May 4, 1864. No later record ★ Holley, J. M. -- Private - April 20, 1861. Received pay July 11, 1862. No later record ★ Hood, Ike A. -- Private - April 20, 1861. Transferred to Company B, 9th Regiment, Georgia Infantry, August 31, 1861. Surrendered, Appomattox, Virginia April 9, 1865 ★ Howell, William H. -- Private - April 20, 1861. Killed, Wilderness, Virginia May 6, 1864 ★ Ingram, S. K. -- Private - April 20, 1861. Appears last on roll for August 31, 1861 ★ Isbell, James P. -- Private - April 20, 1861. Appears last on roll for August 31, 1861 ★ Jackson, J. Shelby -- Private - January 6, 1863. Roll for December 31, 1864, last on file, shows him absent, sent to hospital April 5, 1863 ★ James, William A. -- Private - April 20, 1861. Appears last on roll for August 31, 1861 ★ Johnson, Robert A. -- Private - April 20, 1861. Appointed 3rd Sergeant July 2, 1863. Killed, Wilderness, Virginia May 5, 1864 ★ Kellett, William -- Private - April 20, 1861. Appears last on roll for August 31, 1861 ★ Kelley, Benjamin R. -- Private - April 20, 1861. Transferred to Company A, in 1862. Paroled, Augusta, Georgia May 19, 1865 ★ Ketchum, James S. -- Private - July 1, 1861. Discharged, disability, September 25, 1861. Enlisted as a private, Company A, 36th Regiment, Georgia Infantry, January 15, 1862. Took oath of allegiance to U. S. Government, Chattanooga, Tennessee, and released to remain north of Ohio River during war, May 24, 1864 ★ Lacy, Elijah -- Private - April 20, 1861. Died October 16, 1862 ★ Lacy, Robert -- Private - April 20, 1861. Appears last on roll for August 31, 1861 ★ Lacy, William M. -- Private - April 20, 1861. Discharged, disability, October 18, 1861 ★ Little, R. M. -- 4th Sergeant - April 20, 1861. Elected 2nd Lieutenant December 15, 1862. Killed, Chickamauga, Georgia September 19, 1863 ★ Little, William Bennett -- Private - January 28, 1863. Surrendered, Appomattox, Virginia April 9, 1865 ★ Malloy, James -- 1st Corporal - April 20, 1861. Appears last on roll for August 31, 1861 ★ Malone, A. N. -- Private - April 20, 1861. Appears last on roll for August 31, 1861 ★ Mangrum, W. C. (or Mangum) -- 4th Corporal - April 20, 1861. Appears last on roll for August 31, 1861 ★ Massengale, J. T. -- Private - April 20, 1861. Surrendered, Appomattox, Virginia April 9, 1865 ★ Massengale, Riley N. -- Private - April 20, 1861. Appointed 2nd Sergeant April 28, 1862. Surrendered, Appomattox, Virginia April 9, 1865 ★ Masters, James M. -- Private - April 20, 1861. Authorized to travel from Savannah, Georgia to Richmond, Virginia, to rejoin regiment when physically able to do so, July 31, 1861. No later record ★ Metts, Hugh C. -- Private - April 20, 1861. Appears last on roll for August 31, 1861 ★ Millirons, Henry -- Private - April 20, 1861. Captured in 1862. Received on Steamer Emerald near Vicksburg, Mississippi for exchange November 1, 1862. Admitted to General Field Hospital, Chattanooga, Tennessee with variola, in 1863.

Returned to duty February 17, 1864 ★ Millirons, William J. -- Private - April 20, 1861. Appointed Corporal. Surrendered, Appomattox, Virginia April 9, 1865 ★ Morgan, Jacob L. -- Private - April 20, 1861. Discharged, disability, November 8, 1861. Enlisted as a private, Company A, 36th Regiment, Georgia Infantry, January 15, 1862. Elected Captain, Company I, March 19, 1862. Captured, Vicksburg, Mississippi July 4, 1863, and paroled there July 9, 1863. Killed, Resaca, Georgia May 14, 1864. Buried there ★ Mote, Joseph -- Private - April 20, 1861. Appears last on roll for August 31, 1861 ★ Mote, S. M. P. -- Private - April 20, 1861. Appears last on roll for August 31, 1861 ★ Mote, Silas T. -- Private - April 20, 1861. Appointed 4th Sergeant, Company A, 36th Regiment, Georgia Infantry, January 15, 1862. Captured, Vicksburg, Mississippi July 4, 1863 and paroled there July 9, 1863. No later record ★ Nix, Thomas -- Private - July 1, 1861. Wounded and captured, Gettysburg, Pennsylvania July 2, 1863. Leg amputated in 1863. Paroled, DeCamp General Hospital, David's Island, New York in 1863. Received, City Point, Virginia for exchange September 16, 1863 ★ Overstreet, James S. -- Private - 1862. Wounded in head in 1864. Admitted to Ocmulgee Hospital, Macon, Georgia September 8, 1864. Transferred September 11, 1864. No later record ★ Owen, James – Musician - April 20, 1861. Appears last on roll for August 31, 1861 ★ Perkins, Robert -- Private - April 20, 1861. Appointed 3rd Corporal April 28, 1862. Roll for December 31, 1864, last an file, shows him present ★ Phelan, R. R. -- Private - April 20, 1861. Absent without leave April 6-December 31, 1864 ★ Pilcher, Samuel -- Private - April 20, 1861. Roll for December 31, 1864, last on file, shows him present ★ Pitman, William M. -- 3rd Corporal - April 20, 1861. Elected 1st Lieutenant April 28, 1862; Captain July 2, 1863. Killed, Cold Harbor, Virginia June 1, 1864 ★ Plowman, John T. -- Enlisted as a private in Company B, 9th Regiment, Georgia Infantry, June 12, 1861. Transferred to Company H. 2nd Regiment, Georgia Infantry, August 30, 1862 ★ Pool, R. Jackson -- Private - July 1, 1861. No later record ★ Pope, Ross Kennon -- Private - April 20, 1861. Wounded, Gettysburg, Pennsylvania July 2, 1863. Deserted. Took oath of allegiance to U. S. Government, Chattanooga, Tennessee, May 19, 1864 ★ Roberson, G. W. -- Private - April 20, 1861. Died, Richmond, Virginia July 15, 1862 ★ Roberson, Robert Franklin -- Private - April 20, 1861. Roll for August 31, 1861, shows him present. No later record. Enlisted as a private in Company I, 1st

Regiment, Georgia State Troops, June 1, 1863. Absent without leave March 1864. Dismissed by order A. & I. General's Office. May 1864. Enlisted as a private in Captain Turner's Company, Mississippi Light Artillery April 6, 1864. Roll for June 1864, last on file, shows him present. Surrendered and paroled, Meridian, Mississippi May 10, 1865. Born in 1847. Died at Trion; Georgia in 1924 ★ Sanders, J. W. -- Private - July 1, 1861. Appears last on roll for August 31, 1861 ★ Sansom, John Leonard -- Private - April 20, 1861. Elected Jr. 2nd Lieutenant of Company A, 36th Regiment, Georgia Infantry, January 15, 1862; 2nd Lieutenant September 2, 1862; 1st Lieutenant September 21, 1862. Captured, Vicksburg, Mississippi July 4, 1863, and paroled there July 9, 1863. Resigned, disability, February 14, 1864. (Born in Georgia March 8, 1824.) ★ Seymour, G. W. -- Private - April 20, 1861. Appears last on roll for August 31, 1861 ★ Sinor, John -- Private - April 20, 1861. Received pay at Richmond, Virginia August 13, 1862. No later record ★ Smallwood, Jesse -- Private - April 20, 1861. Died, fever, Richmond, Virginia August 15, 1861. Buried there in Hollywood Cemetery ★ Smith, W. W. -- Private - July 1, 1861. Appears last on roll for August 31, 1861 ★ Smith, Wesley A. – Musician - April 20, 1861. Killed, Malvern Hill, Virginia June 30, 1862 ★ Sosman, G. W. (or Sasman) -- Private - January 24, 1863. Deserted September 19, 1863 ★ Stafford, George W. -- Private - April 20, 1861. Discharged August 1862. Enlisted as a private, Company G, 4th Regiment, Georgia Cavalry, (Avery's), April 1863. Captured, Sweetwater, Tennessee July 1, 1864. Released, Camp Douglas, Illinois June 16, 1865 ★ Stafford, N. A. -- 1st Sergeant - April 20, 1861. Appointed Brevet 2nd Lieutenant in 1861. Appears last on roll for August 31, 1861 ★ Sutton, Andrew J. -- Private - April 20, 1861. Roll for December 31, 1864, last on file, shows him present ★ Talley, John W. -- Private - April 20, 1861. Appears last an roll for August 31, 1861 ★ Thrailkill, G. W. -- Private - April 20, 1861. Appears last on roll for August 31, 1861 ★ Vandergriff, J. R. -- Private - April 20, 1861. Appears last on roll for August 31, 1861 ★ Vandergriff, James A. -- Private - April 20, 1861. Appears last on roll for August 31, 1861 ★ West, Joseph M. -- Private - April 20, 1861. Appears last on roll for August 3

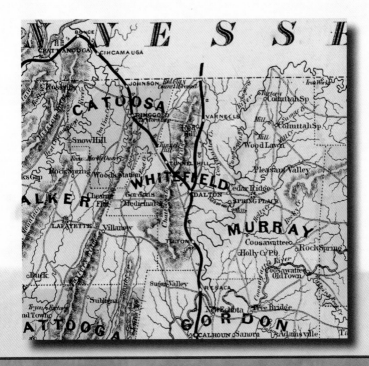

COMPANY I, 2ND REGIMENT
MARION COUNTY "BUENA VISTA GUARDS"

Anderson, George W. -- Private - April 15, 1861. Surrendered, Appomattox, Virginia April 9, 1865 ★ Ashmore, Albert G. -- Private - April 15, 1861. Sick in hospital August 31, 1861. No later record ★ Belk, Joseph T. -- Private - April 15, 1861. Wounded; finger amputated. Roll for December 31, 1864, last on file, shows him on detached duty ★ Belk, Zack -- Private - April 15, 1861. Paid for commutation of rations while on furlough March 27, 1863. No later record ★ Bell, E. J. -- Private - July 14, 1861. Died April 20, 1862 ★ Benson, J. L -- Private - August 8, 1861. Surrendered, Appomattox, Virginia April 9, 1865 ★ Bigham, Samuel -- Private - April 15, 1861. Appears last on roll for August 31, 1861 ★ Birdsong, C. W. -- Private - July 14, 1861. Appointed Sergeant. Wounded in Virginia June 27, 1862. Paid for commutation of rations March 17, 1863. No later record ★ Bowling, E. H. (or Bolan) -- Private. Paroled, Augusta, Georgia May 18, 1865 ★ Braddy, John M. (or J. J.) -- Private. Appointed Corporal. Paroled, Augusta, Georgia May 18, 1865 ★ Brasington, James L. (or Brassington) -- 4th Sergeant - April 15, 1861. Appears last on roll for August 31, 1861 ★ Brooks, Robert D. -- Private - April 15, 1861. Died July 1, 1862 ★ Brown, Reuben -- Private - April 15, 1861. Discharged October 24, 1861. Elected 2nd Lieutenant of Company G, 10th Regiment, Georgia State Troops, December 16, 1861. Mustered out May 1862. Enlisted as a private, Company G, 59th Regiment, Georgia Infantry, May 6, 1862. Elected 1st Lieutenant November 1, 1862. Wounded, Petersburg, Virginia, September 1864. Furloughed for 30 days from Jackson Hospital, Richmond, Virginia November 23, 1864. In Richmond, Virginia hospital, wounded, close of war ★ Buckner, C. R. -- Private - July 8, 1861. Home on furlough August 31, 1861. No later record ★ Bullock, James H. -- 2nd Corporal - April 15, 1861. Died July 16, 1862 ★ Butt, Richard E. -- Private - April 15, 1861. Died, typhoid fever, Camp Pine Creek, Virginia, September 29, 1861 ★ Butt, William B. -- Private - April 15, 1861. Appointed Sergeant in 1861. Discharged, disability, October 29, 1861 ★ Butt, William H. -- 3rd Corporal - April 15, 1861. Appears last on roll for August 31, 1861 ★ Calhoun, James G. -- Jr. 2nd Lieutenant - April 15, 1861. Resigned August 30, 1861 ★ Calhoun, James G. -- Private - April 15, 1861. Appears last on roll for August 31, 1861 ★ Cater, James (or Cato) -- Private - April 15, 1861. Appears last on roll for August 31, 1861 ★ Cato, John W. R. -- Private - April 15, 1861. Transferred to Regimental Band June 1, 1861. Appointed 2nd Sergeant. Deserted to enemy September 20, 1864. Received by Provost Marshal General, Defenses South of Potomac, Washington, D. C., September 24, 1864. Took oath of allegiance to U. S. Government and sent to Fairfield, Conn., September 24, 1864 ★ Chambless, Henry B. -- Private - April 15, 1861. Elected 2nd Lieutenant July 1, 1862. Surrendered, Appomattox, Virginia April 9, 1865 ★ Cottingham, John T. -- 3rd Sergeant - April 15, 1861. Home on sick furlough August 31, 1861. No later record ★ Crew, Eli A -- 1st Corporal - April 15, 1861. On duty as Enrolling Officer, Marion County, Georgia, December 31, 1864. No later record ★ Davis, D. A. -- Private - July 8, 1861. Discharged, Richmond, Virginia between July 8 and August 31, 1861 ★ Dowd, Andrew H. -- Private - April 15, 1861. Appointed 1st Sergeant. Received pay May 17, 1862. No later record ★ Dudley, George H. -- Private - April 15, 1861. Discharged, disability, Brooks' Station, Virginia July or August 1861. Elected Jr. 2nd Lieutenant of Company G, 10th Regiment, Georgia State Troops, December 16, 1861. Mustered out May 1862. Elected Jr. 2nd Lieutenant of Company H, 59th Regiment, Georgia Infantry, May 6, 1862. Wounded at Gettysburg, Pennsylvania July 3, 1863. Died August 27, 1863. Buried in Thornrose Cemetery at Staunton, Virginia ★ Edge, Jehu -- Private - August 8, 1861. Discharged, disability, August 24, 1861. Enlisted as a private in Company E, 3rd Regiment, Georgia Cavalry, April 28, 1862. Wounded near Murfreesboro, Tennessee. Captured at Cumberland Mountain or McMinnville, Tennessee, October 3, 1863. Transferred from Rock Island, Illinois for exchange March 20, 1865. Received at Boulware &

Cox's Wharves, James River, Virginia, March 27, 1865. Died in Madison County, Georgia, September 25, 1903 ★ Farr, John B. -- 1st Sergeant - April 15, 1861. Appears last on roll for July 1, 1861 ★ Fulford, William -- Private - April 15, 1861. Discharged, disability, November 25, 1861 ★ Gunn, Wilson L. -- Private - April 15, 1861. Died at Yatesville, North Carolina April 28, 1863 ★ Guy, Walter T. -- Private - July 14, 1861. Surrendered, Appomattox, Virginia April 9, 1865 ★ Guy, William J. -- Private - April 15, 1861. Surrendered, Tallahassee, Florida May 10, 1865. Paroled, Albany, Georgia May 17, 1865 ★ Halley, J. M. -- Private - July 14, 1861. Discharged, disability, December 5, 1861 ★ Halley, N. D. -- Private - July 14, 1861. Wounded in 1862. Died, wounds, Hospital # 4, Wilmington, North Carolina, July 21, 1862 ★ Halley, N. T. -- Private - July 14, 1861. Appears last on roll for August 31, 1861 ★ Hardison, Franklin L. -- Private - April 15, 1861. Elected 2nd Lieutenant April 28, 1862. Killed, Malvern Hill, Virginia July 1, 1862 ★ Harrold, John J. (or Harrell) -- Private - May 5, 1861. Surrendered, Appomattox, Virginia April 9, 1865 ★ Hertz, Jacob Herman -- Private - April 15, 1861. Discharged, exempt from service, July 11, 1862 ★ Hester, Joseph L. (or Joseph J.) -- Private - July 14, 1861. Surrendered, Appomattox, Virginia April 9, 1865 ★ Horn, Joel G. -- Private - April 15, 1861. Home on sick furlough August 31, 1861. No later record ★ Horn, Levi -- Private - April 15, 1861. Died October 17, 1861 ★ Ivey, Joseph C. -- Private - April 15, 1861. Paid commutation of rations for period September 3, 1862 -February 21, 1863, on August 24, 1863. No later record ★ Johnston, William R. -- Private. Surrendered, Tallahassee, Florida May 10, 1865. Paroled, Albany, Georgia May 17, 1865 ★ Josey, J. T. -- Private - August 8, 1861. In Richmond, Virginia hospital August 31, 1861. No later record ★ Kemp, Larkin B. -- Private - April 15, 1861. Died in 1862 ★ Kendrick, John A. -- Private - April 15, 1861. Elected 2nd Lieutenant, Company C, 37th Regiment Alabama Infantry August 5, 1862. On roster dated December 31, 1864, name appears with remark as to date and cause of vacancy "P. August 2, 1864." ★ Kennerly, William W. -- Private - April 15, 1861. Elected Jr. 2nd Lieutenant April 28, 1862. Wounded and captured, Gettysburg, Pennsylvania July 5, 1863. Elected 1st Lieutenant October 8, 1863. Paroled, Johnson's Island, Ohio, March 1865. Received, Cox's Wharf James River, Virginia for exchange March 22, 1865 ★ Lowe, James William -- Private - April 15, 1861. Transferred to Regimental Band July 10, 1861. Wounded; leg amputated. Discharged, having been elected to civil office, May 21, 1864 ★ Maddox, John T. -- 2nd Lieutenant - April 15, 1861. Elected Captain April 28, 1862. Resigned October 8, 1863 ★ Mason, L. B. -- Private - April 15, 1861. Appointed Hospital Steward June 1, 1861. Surrendered, Appomattox, Virginia April 9, 1865 ★ Mathis, Brittan H. -- Private - April 15, 1861. Appointed Sergeant June 7, 1861. Appears last on roll for August 31, 1864 ★ Mathis, Harvey G. -- Private - April 15, 1861. Absent on indefinite furlough July 1, 1861. No later record ★ McCarroll, Perryman -- Private - October 21, 1864. Surrendered, Appomattox, Virginia April 9, 1865 ★ McMichael, John -- Private - April 15, 1861. Appears last on roll for August 31, 1861 ★ McMichael, Seaborn W. -- Private - April 15, 1861. Received pay while on furlough at Richmond, Virginia for period July 1-August 31, 1861, on September 13, 1861. No later record ★ McPherson, T. D. -- Private - July 8, 1861. Appears last on roll for August 31, 1861 ★ Monk, Silas -- Private - April 15, 1861. At home on sick furlough August 31, 1861 ★ Moore, Dunbar -- Private - April 15, 1861. Appears last on roll for August 31, 1861 ★ Moore, John -- Private - April 15, 1861. Took oath of allegiance to U. S. Government, released and furnished transportation to Philadelphia, Pennsylvania, October 10, 1864 ★ Norman, James T. -- Private - July 14, 1861. Paid for period January 1-June 30, 1862, on July 19, 1862. No later record ★ Oliver, Thaddeus -- Private - April 15, 1861. Admitted to Chimborazo Hospital # 1, Richmond, Virginia, March 21, 1862. Elected Captain, Company E, 63rd Regiment, Georgia Infantry, December

11, 1862. Resigned May 29, 1863. Elected 1st Lieutenant, Company D, 28th Battalion, Georgia Siege Artillery, August 6, 1863. Wounded John's Island, South Carolina July 1864, and died there, wounds, August 20, 1864 ★ O'Tyson, J. H. H. -- Private - August 8, 1861. Appears last on roll for August 31, 1861 ★ Owen, George W. -- Private - July 14, 1861. Died, Richmond, Virginia September 27, 1861 ★ Patrick, William J. -- Private - August 8, 1861. Discharged, disability, October 26, 1861 ★ Paul, Jabez M. -- Private - August 8, 1861. Discharged, disability, November 6, 1861 ★ Paul, John -- Private - April 15, 1861. Appears last on roll for August 31, 1861 ★ Pearson, E. P. -- Private - April 15, 1861. Transferred to Company I, 17th Regiment, Georgia Infantry, July 1862. On furlough February 28, 1865. Furloughed for 30 days at Petersburg, Virginia March 12, 1865 ★ Peebles, Francis G. M. -- Private - June 20, 1861. Appears last on roll for August 31, 1861 ★ Peebles, I. H. -- 1st Lieutenant - April 15, 1861. Appears last on roll for August 31, 1861 ★ Phillips, Benjamin F. -- Private - July 24, 1861. Lost eye, Chickamauga, Georgia, September 19, 1863. Roll for December 31, 1864, last on file, shows him present ★ Powell, James M. -- Private - April 15, 1861. Captured, Vicksburg, Mississippi July 3, 1863. Received, Pt. Lookout, Maryland October 20, 1863, and died there February 25, 1864 ★ Rogers, A. J. -- Private - July 14, 1861. In Richmond, Virginia hospital August 31, 1861. No later record ★ Rushin, John R. -- Private - April 15, 1861. Discharged, disability, November 25, 1861. Elected 2nd Lieutenant, Company H, 46th Regiment, Georgia Infantry, March 4, 1862. Wounded, Chickamauga, Georgia, September. 20, 1863. Retired to Invalid Corps December 15, 1864 ★ Ryan, James Waters -- Private - June 28, 1861. Transferred to Regimental Band July 25, 1861; to C. S. Navy September 17, 1864. Served at Wilmington, North Carolina 1863-1864. Born Waterford, Ireland September 25, 1836 ★ Sanders, W. J. -- Private - July 14, 1861. Appears last on roll for August 31, 1861 ★ Scogin, Richard W. -- Private - April 15, 1861. Captured, Dandridge, Tennessee January 17, 1864. Released, Rock Island, Illinois June 21, 1865 ★ Scogins, L. H. -- Private - July 14, 1861. Absent, waiting on brother at hospital. August 31, 1861. No later record ★ Sheppard, John Abner -- Private - June 20, 1861. Wounded in Virginia June 27, 1862. Paid at Richmond, Virginia for period January 1-June 30, 1862, on July 2, 1862. Elected Jr. 2nd Lieutenant, Company E, 63rd Regiment, Georgia Infantry, December 11, 1862; 2nd Lieutenant May 28, 1863; Captain July 22, 1864. Furloughed February 1865. On detail duty March 1, 1865 to close of war. Born in Georgia in 1841 ★ Shipp, James R. -- Private - April 15, 1861. Appears last on roll for August 31, 1861 ★ Slaughter, John W. -- Private - May 5, 1861. Appointed 1st Sergeant. Shot twice in left hand, resulting in amputation of finger, Wilderness, Virginia May 6, 1864. Absent, wounded, December 31, 1864. Surrendered, Tallahassee, Florida May 10, 1865. Paroled, Albany, Georgia May 16, 1865. Died Atlanta, Georgia September 9, 1895 ★ Smith, John T. -- Private - April 15, 1861. Appears last on roll for August 31, 1861 ★ Smith, William T. -- Private - April 15, 1861. Surrendered, Appomattox, Virginia April 9, 1865 ★ Statham, M. D. -- Private - July 24, 1861. Appears last on roll for August 31, 1861 ★ Stokes, William -- Private - May 5, 1861. Roll for December 31, 1864, last on file, shows him absent on Surgeon's certificate ★ Story, Joseph -- Private - August 28, 1861. Appears last on roll for August 31, 1861 ★ Story, Josiah P. -- Private - April 15, 1861. Died Richmond, Virginia November 11, 1861 ★ Story, William -- Private - April 15, 1861. At home, sick, August 31, 1861. No later record ★ Tamplin, William H. -- Private - April 15, 1861. Appears last on roll for July 1, 1861 ★ Tidd, Mathew M. -- Private - April 15, 1861. Wounded, Wilderness, Virginia May 6, 1864; Seven Days Fight near Richmond, Virginia June 20, 1864. Surrendered, Tallahassee, Florida May 10, 1865. Paroled, Albany, Georgia May 22, 1865 ★ Toney, H. M. -- Private - August 8, 1861. Appears last on roll for August 31, 1861 ★ Upton, G. S. -- Private - August 8, 1861. Severely wounded, Wilderness, Virginia, May 6, 1864. Surrendered, Tallahassee, Florida May 10, 1865. Paroled, Albany, Georgia May 18, 1865 ★ Upton, R. M. -- Private - August 8, 1861. In Culpeper Court House, Virginia hospital August 31, 1861. No later record ★ Wall, Carey J. -- Private - April 15, 1861. Died September 12, 1861 ★ Watkins, J. B. -- Private - July 14, 1861. Surrendered, Appomattox, Virginia April 9, 1865 ★ Watts, H. C. -- Private - July 14, 1861. Appointed Sergeant. Captured, Richmond, Virginia hospital April 3, 1865. Transferred to Pt. Lookout, Maryland May 2, 1865 ★ Watts, M. B. -- Enlisted as a private, Company G, 10th Regiment, Georgia State Troops, December 16, 1861. Mustered out May 1862. Enlisted as a private, Company H, 59th Regiment, Georgia Infantry, May 6, 1862. Transferred to Company I, 17th Regiment, Georgia Infantry, in exchange for John A. Shierling, Jr., February 24, 1863. Transferred to Company I, 2nd Regiment, Georgia Infantry, March 1, 1863. No later record ★ Webb, Lewis -- 2nd Sergeant - April 15, 1861. Received pay at Richmond, Virginia for period August 1, 1861 -April 15, 1862, on December 11, 1862. No later record ★ Wiggins, Charles R -- Captain - April 15, 1861. Appears last on roll for August 31, 1861 ★ Wiggins, James W. -- 4th Corporal - April 15, 1861. Received pay at Richmond, Virginia for period January 1-April 30, 1862, on May 20, 1862. No later record ★ Wiggins, Jasper M. -- Private - April 15, 1861. Killed, Wilderness, Virginia May 6, 1864 ★ Windsor, N. A. -- Private - July 14, 1861. Surrendered, Tallahassee, Florida May 10, 1865. Paroled, Albany, Georgia May 17, 1865 ★ Windsor, R. S. -- Private - July 14, 1861. Appears last on roll for August 31, 1861 ★ Wisdom, F. L. -- Private - April 15, 1861. Elected Captain October 8, 1863. Wounded in foot, Wilderness, Virginia, May 6, 1864. Furloughed account of wounds March 31, 1865 ★ Wooten, Cullen H. -- Private - April 15, 1861. Transferred to Regimental Band June 25, 1861. Left Chimborazo Hospital, Richmond, Virginia, without permission ★ Wyatt, Phillip H. -- Private - April 15, 1861. Appears last on roll for August 31, 1861 ★ Wyatt, W. W. -- Private - August 8, 1861. In Culpeper Court House, Virginia hospital August 31, 1861. No later record.

COMPANY K, 2ND REGIMENT
GEORGIA VOLUNTEER INFANTRY
STEWART COUNTY "STEWART GREYS"

Ball, Jared J. (or Jared I.)--Captain July 17, 1861. appears last on roll for Oct. 1861. Resigned ★ Gillis, Malcolm--1st Lieutenant July 17, 1861. Resigned 1862. Elected 1st Lieutenant, Co. G, 46th Regt. Ga. Inf. Mar. 4, 1862; Captain July 30, 1862. Acting Field Officer July - Aug. 1864. Surrendered, Greensboro, N.C. Apr. 26, 1865 ★ Richardson, William C.--2d Lieutenant July 17, 1861. Died, Warrenton, Va. Oct. 23, 1861 ★ Newell, Joseph B.--Jr. 2d Lieutenant July 17, 1861. Elected Captian Dec. 9, 1863. Furloughed from Ocmulgee Hospital, Macon, Ga. Mar. 27, 1865 ★ Rockwell, Henry L.--1st Sergeant July 17, 1861. Elected 1st Lieutenant Apr. 28, 1862. Captured, Green Castle, Pa. July 5, 1863. Paroled, JohnsonÕs Island, O. and forwarded to Pt. Lookout, Md. for exchange Mar. 14, 1865. Received, Cox's Wharf, James River, Va. Mar. 22, 1865 ★ Boynton, William W.--2d Sergeant July 17, 1861. Elected 2d Lieutenant Apr. 28 1862. Killed, Sharpsburg, Md. Sept. 17, 1862 ★ Gregory, P.H.--3d Sergeant July 17, 1861. Transferred to Co. C, 19th Battn. Ga. Cavalry and elected 2d Lieutenant July 24, 1862. Transferred to Co. I, 19th Regt. Confederate Cavalry and elected 1st Lieutenant. Paroled, Hillsboro, N.C. May 3, 1865 ★ Singer, Joseph E.--4th Sergeant July 17, 1861. Transferred to Regimental Band. Surrendered, Appomattox, Va. Apr. 9, 1865 ★ Lowrey, John W.F.--1st Corporal July 17, 1861. Discharged July 1862. Elected Lieutenant, Co. K, 11th Regt. Ga. Militia July 22, 1864; Captain 1864. Paroled, Thomasville, Ga. Apr. 1865 ★ West, Thomas--2d Corporal July 17, 1861. discharged, disability, Nov. 8, 1861 ★ Collier, Probert--3d Corporal July 17, 1861. Wounded. Elected Captain. Surrendered, Appomattox, Va. Apr. 9, 1865 ★ McMillan, John Thomas (or T.J.)--4th Corporal July 17, 1861. Elected Jr. 2d Lieutenant Dec. 9, 1863. Captured, Ft. Harrison, Va. Sept. 29, 1864. Released, Ft. Delaware, Del. June 17, 1865 ★ Coppedge, John T.--Musician Aug. 7, 1861. Transferred to Regimental Band Aug. 1861. Paid for commutation of rations while on sick leave Mar. 1-31, 1862, on Mar. 26, 1863. No later record ★ Adams, Charles B.--Private July 17, 1861. Appointed Corporal. Sick in hospital Dec. 31, 1864. No later record ★ Adams, R.F.--Private Aug. 16, 1862. Surrendered, Appomattox, Va. Apr. 9, 1865 ★ Adams, Samuel O.--Private July 17, 1861. Transferred to Co. F, 3d Regt. Ga. Inf. and appointed Sergeant May 10, 1862. Transferred to Co. K, same regiment July 26, 1862. No later record ★ Alexander, J.D.--Private Sept. 17, 1861. Appears last on roll for Oct. 31, 1861 ★ Allen, William--Private Feb. 22, 1863. Captured, Gettysburg, Pa. July 3, 1863. Died, Pt. Lookout, Md. Feb. 1, 1864 ★ Ard, G.W.--Private Sept. 17, 1861. Wounded in right leg, resulting in amputation, Sharpsburg, Md. Sept. 17, 1862. Paroled, Ft. McHenry, Md. and sent to Ft. Monroe, Va. for exchange May 17, 1863 ★ Armour, J.B.--Private Aug. 12, 1861. Sick in Richmond, Va. hospital Oct. 6, 1861. No later record ★ Baker, J.T.--Private Dec. 2, 1863. Surrendered, Appomattox, Va. Apr. 9, 1865 ★ Ball, Green A.--Private July 17, 1861. Discharged, disability, Richmond, Va. Sept. 4, 1861. Elected Captain, Co. K, 46th Regt. Ga. Inf. Mar. 4, 1862. Resigned Charleston, S.C. July 30, 1862 ★ Barefield, Samuel W. (or Barfield)--Private July 17, 1861. Sick in hospital Dec. 31, 1864. No later record ★ Barefield, W. Henry (or Barfield)--Private Feb. 22, 1863. Surrendered, Appomattox, Va. Apr. 9, 1865 ★ Barfield, Jasper R. (or Barefield)--Private Dec. 2, 1863. Surrendered, Appomattox, Va. Apr. 9, 1865. Died, Albany, Ga. Apr. 4, 1926 ★ Bartlett, James M.--Private July 17, 1861. Admitted to C.S.A. General Hospital, Charlottesville, Va. Nov. 11, 1861. Sent to General Hospital, Lynchburg, Va. Apr. 23, 1862. Died Atlanta, Ga. Oct. 18, 1863. Buried there Oakland Cemetery ★ Bartlett, T.J.--Private Dec. 2, 1863. Surrendered, Appomattox, Va. Apr. 9, 1865 ★ Beall, Samuel--Private July 17, 1861. Elected 2d Lieutenant Sept. 17, 1862. Resigned Nov. 6, 1862 or Oct. 1, 1863 ★ Blount, W.H.L.--Private Sept. 17, 1861. Sick in Richmond, Va. hospital Oct. 19, 1861. No later record ★ Bowers, David--Private July 17, 1861. Died Sept. 15, 1862

★ Boynton, J.L.--Private July 17, 1861. Appointed 4th Corporal 1861; Sergeant 1861. Discharged, Richmond, Va. Oct. 18, 1861 ★ Braswell, Jacob--Private Apr. 25, 1864. Furloughed for 20 days from Aug. 6, 1864. Absent without leave Aug. 31, 1864. "Deserted and advertised by order of Gen. Cobb" Jan.-Feb. 1865 ★ Bridges, Thomas J.--Private July 17, 1861. Appointed Corporal. Surrendered, Appomattox, Va. Apr. 9, 1865 ★ Brown, M.J.--Private July 17, 1861. Sick in Richmond, Va. Hospital Oct. 16, 1861. No later record ★ Bryan, N.R.--Private July 17, 1861. Discharged, account of tuberculosis, Dec. 22, 1861 ★ Chestnut, A.J.--Private Sept. 17, 1861. Discharged, disability, Dec. 14, 1861 ★ Chestnut, Charles W. Jr.--Private Sept. 17, 1861. Absent, sick, Oct. 6-31, 1861. Transferred to Co. E, 31st Regt. Ga. Inf. in exchange for D.B. Elliott Sept. 26, 1862. Died, smallpox, Hospital of 2d Corps, Guinea Station, Va. Jan. 30, 1863 ★ Crocker, Allen--Private July 17, 1861. Captured, Ft. Harrison, Va. Sept. 30, 1864. Paroled, Pt. Lookout, Md. for exchanged Mar. 1865. Received, Boulware's Wharf, James River, Va. Mar. 19, 1865 ★ Crocker, E. T.--Private July 17, 1861. Admitted to General Hospital, Charlottesville, Va. Sept. 4, 1862. Sent to General Hospital, Lynchburg, Va. Sept. 5, 1862. Killed, Chickamauga, Ga. Sept. 19, 1863 ★ Crocker, Thomas--Private July 17, 1861. Appears last on roll for Oct. 31, 1861 ★ Crocker, W.H.--Private July 17, 1861. Wounded, Chickamauga, Ga. Sept, 19, 1863. Wounded and disabled, Spotsylvania, Va. May 12, 1864. Surrendered, Tallahassee, Fla. May 10, 1865. Paroled, Albany, Ga. May 17, 1865 ★ Davis, J.K.--Private July 17, 1861. Transferred to Co. G, 46th Regt. Ga. Inf. July 22, 1862. Surrendered, Greensboro, N.C. Apr. 26, 1865 ★ Davis, W.J.--Private July 17, 1861. Surrendered, Appomattox, Va. Apr. 9, 1865 ★ Dossett, W.J.--Private July 17, 1861. Surrendered, Appomattox, Va. Apr. 9, 1865 ★ Duskin, Mich. T.--Private July 17, 1861. Appointed Sergeant. Paroled, Albany, Ga. May 17, 1865 ★ Duskin, William Jackson--Enlisted as a private, Co. G, 46th Regt. Ga. Inf. Apr. 24, 1862. Transferred to Co. K, 2d Regt. Ga. Inf. July 22, 1862. Died Oct. 23, 1864 ★ Dye, William H.--Private July 17, 1861. Died, Warrenton, Va. Nov. 18, 1861 ★ Edwards, G.W.--Private Sept. 17, 1861. Died Nov. 22, 1861 ★ Elliott, David Benjamin--Enlisted as a private, Co. E, 31st Regt. Ga. Inf. Nov. 13, 1861. Transferred to Co. K, 2d Regt. Ga. Inf. in exchange for Charles W. Chestnut Jr. Sept. 26, 1862. Surrendered, Appomattox, Va. Apr. 9, 1865 ★ Farnham, J.W.--Private Oct. 1, 1861. Sick at Manassas, Va. Oct. 31, 1861. No later record ★ Fitzgerald, William Walton--Private July 17, 1861. Sick at Richmond, Va. Oct. 16, 1861 ★ Flynn, W.D.--Private Aug. 13, 1861. Sent to Main Street Hospital, Richmond, Va. Sept. 10, 1861. Enlisted as a private, Co. G, 46th Regt. Ga. Inf. Apr. 24, 1862. Surrendered, Greensboro, N.C. Apr. 26, 1865 ★ Folks, J.B.--Private July 17, 1861. Surrendered, Appomattox, Va. Apr. 9, 1865 ★ Folks, R.C.--Private July 17, 1861. Appears last on roll for Oct. 31, 1861 ★ Fort, Tomlinson--Private July 17, 1861. Discharged, disability, Sept 12, 1861. Appointed 4th Corporal, Co. G, 46th Regt. Ga. Inf. Mar. 4, 1862. Appointed Musician Aug. 1862. Died, Cassville, Ga. Jan. 21, 1864 ★ Garrett, B.F.--Private July 17, 1861. Killed near Richmond, Va. June 27, 1862 ★ Giddins, J.M.--Private Feb. 22, 1863. Surrendered, Appomattox, Va. Apr. 9, 1865 ★ Grimes, R.J.--Private July 17, 1861. Surrendered, Appomattox, Va. Apr. 9, 1865 ★ Hadden, Daniel--Private July 17, 1861. Died Feb. 19, 1862 ★ Hadden, Josiah B.--Private Sept. 17, 1861. Died Feb. 17, 1862 ★ Halliday, D.W.--Private July 17, 1861. Died, Manassas, Va. Mar. 6, 1862 ★ Halliday, G.R.--Private July 17, 1861. Appears last on roll for Oct. 31, 1861 ★ Halliday, T.H.--Private Oct. 1, 1861. Appears last on roll for Oct. 31, 1861 ★ Hardwick, W.P.--Private July 17, 1861. Wounded 1862. Admitted to General Hospital, wounded, Oct. 10, 1862. Transferred to Burk's Cavalry, Forrest's Command June 30, 1864 ★ Hilliard, Andrew J.B.--Private Sept. 17, 1861. Died Nov. 10, 1861

★ Hilliard, A.P.--Private Sept. 17, 1861. Sick in Richmond, Va. Oct. 16, 1861. No later record ★ Hillsman, William C.--Private July 17, 1861. Received pay June 30, 1863. No later record ★ Hines, B.R.--Private July 17, 1861. Elected 2d Lieutenant Oct. 1, 1863. Roll for Dec. 31, 1864, last on file, shows him present ★ House, W.H.--Private July 17, 1861. Surrendered, Appomattox, Va. Apr. 9, 1865 ★ Humber, Charles Christian--Private Sept. 17, 1861. Elected 2d Lieutenant Oct. 29, 1861. Retired Apr. 28, 1862. Elected Captain Co. E, 11th Regt. Ga. Militia July 1864. Wounded at Atlanta, Ga. July 22, 1864. Surrendered, Doctortown, Ga. May 1865 ★ Hurley, James H.--Private July 17, 1861. Wounded 2d Manassas, Va. Aug. 30, 1862. Died, wounds and typhoid pneumonia, Sept. 20, 1862 ★ Jackson, M.G.--Private Sept. 17, 1861. Died prior to Sept. 30, 1862 ★ Jackson, R.D.--Private July 17, 1861. Paroled, Lynchburg, Va. Apr. 15, 1865 ★ Jarrell, E.H.--Private July 17, 1861. Wounded, Wilderness, Va. May 6, 1864. Retired to Invalid Corps Nov. 7, 1864. Assigned to light duty with Brigadier General Gardner Dec. 3, 1864 ★ Johnson, William W.--Private Apr. 25, 1864. Roll for Feb. 28, 1865, shows him present ★ Kidd, T.J.--Private Sept. 17, 1861. Discharged, disability, Nov. 24, 1864 ★ Lavan, Timothy--Private July 17, 1861. Captured Falling Waters, Md. July 14, 1863. Took oath of allegiance to U.S. Govt., Old Capitol Prison, Washington, D.C. and released Dec. 13, 1863 ★ Lewisford, J.P.--Private Aug. 13, 1861. Absent, sick, Richmond, Va. Oct. 31, 1861. No later record ★ Lowe, G.W.--Private July 17, 1861. Appears last on roll for Oct. 31, 1861 ★ Lowe, John T.--Private July 17, 1861. Wounded in leg, resulting in amputation, Wilderness, Va. May 6, 1864. Home on wounded furlough close of war ★ Mansfield, J.B.--Private July 17, 1861. Furloughed Feb. 11, 1865 ★ Martin, W.H.--Private July 17, 1861. Appointed Corporal. Surrendered, Appomattox, Va. Apr. 9, 1865 ★ Mathewson, Aaron D. (or Mathison)--Private Aug. 16, 1862. Captured, Amelia Court House, Va. Apr. 4, 1865. Released, Pt. Lookout, Md. June 29, 1865 ★ Mattox, J.M.--Private. Surrendered, Appomattox, Va. Apr. 9, 1865 ★ McCuller, M.C.--Private July 17, 1861. Appointed Sergeant. Paid for arresting deserters, Decatur, Ga. June 22, 1863. No later record ★ McGary, T.J. (or MacGarie)--Private July 17, 1861. Admitted to Chimborazo Hospital #3, Richmond, Va. Apr. 28, 1862. Returned to duty May 17, 1862. No later record ★ Middleton, Charles W.--Private July 17, 1861. Discharged, Richmond, Va. Sept. 30, 1861. Enlisted as a private in Co. E, 31st Regt. Ga. Inf. May 1, 1864. Captured, Petersburg, Va. Mar. 25, 1865. Released, Pt. Lookout, Md. May 14, 1865. Born Stewart County, Ga. May 4, 1841. Died, Albany, Ga. Dec. 21, 1917 ★ Moore, F.M.F.--Private July 17, 1861. Roll dated Aug. 31, 1864, last of file, shows he was transferred ★ Moore, H.C.--Private July 17, 1861. Sick in Richmond, Va. Oct. 16, 1861. No later record ★ Moore, W.J.--Private July 17, 1861. Died Dec. 1, 1861 ★ Nicholson, Robert--Private Jan. 1863. Captured near Jonesboro, Ga. Sept. 1, 1864. Exchanged, Rough & Ready, Ga. Sept. 19-22, 1864. Wounded Nov. 1864. No later record ★ Parham, B.F.--Private July 17, 1861. Roll for Dec. 31, 1864, last on file, shows him present ★ Parker, T.H.--Private July 17, 1861. Surrendered, Appomattox, Va. Apr. 9, 1865 ★ Perkins, G.W.--Private July 17, 1861. Paid for commutation of rations while disabled for period July 5, 1862 - Jan. 5, 1863, on Aug. 25, 1863. No later record ★ Perry, John T.--Private July 17, 1861. Roll for Aug. 31, 1864, shows him present ★ Powell, H.M. (or W.H.)--Private July 17, 1861. Wounded, Wilderness, Va. May 6, 1864. Surrendered, Appomattox, Va. Apr. 9, 1865 ★ Powell, James H. (or J.M.)--Private July 17, 1861. Appointed Ordnance Sergeant July 1861. Surrendered, Appomattox, Va. Apr. 9, 1865 ★ Prestley, M.--Private Sept. 17, 1861. Sent to Mt. Jackson, sick, Oct. 6, 1861. No later record ★ Ramey, John A.--Private July 17, 1861. Appointed Corporal. Killed May 30, 1864 ★ Ramey, S.H.--Private July 17, 1861. Transferred to Co. C. Surrendered, Appomattox, Va. Apr. 9, 1865 ★ Redding, J.L.--Private July 17, 1861. Appointed 2d Sergeant Apr. 28, 1862. Wounded, Wilderness, Va. May 6, 1864. Surrendered, Appomattox, Va. Apr. 9, 1865 ★ Rhodes, G.A.--Private Sept. 17, 1861. Discharged Nov. 24, 1861 ★ Rice, B.W.--Private July 17, 1861. Appointed 3d Sergeant July 24, 1862 ★ Surrendered, Appomattox, Va. Apr. 9, 1865 ★ Richardson, C.W.--Private Sept. 17, 1861. Died May 1862. Buried in Confederate Cemetery at Lynchburg, Va. May 29, 1862. "No. 10, 5th Line, Lot 171, Ferguson's Factory." ★ Seay, John A.--Private July 17, 1861. Absent, sick, Richmond, Va. Sept. 4, 1861. No later record ★ Seay, W.D.--Private July 17, 1861. Surrendered, Appomattox, Va. Apr. 9, 1865 ★ Seymour, G.S.--Private July 17, 1861. Appointed Regimental Assistant Surgeon June 1864; Assistant Surgeon, P.A.C.S. Paroled, Meridian, Miss. May 10, 1865 ★ Seymour, L.S.--Private July 17, 1861. Absent without leave Dec. 31, 1864 ★ Sherman, R.J.--Private July 17, 1861. "Detailed for special duty by order of General Smith

(Batteries)" in 1861. No later record ★ Simpson, C.D.--Private Aug. 16, 1862. Wounded May 1863. Paroled, Burkeville, Va. Apr. 14-17, 1865 ★ Simpson, Thomas--Private July 17, 1861. Appointed Regimental Musician. Surrendered, Appomattox, Va. Apr. 9, 1865 ★ Sinclair, M.D.--Private Oct. 16, 1861. Discharged, Richmond, Va. Oct. 16, 1861 ★ Singer, George--Private July 17, 1861. At Richmond, Va., sick, Aug. 24 - Oct. 31, 1861. No later record ★ Smith, S.T.--Private July 17, 1861. Appointed 4th Sergeant. Surrendered, Appomattox, Va. Apr. 9, 1865 ★ Smelling, J.W.--Private July 17, 1861. Appears last on roll for Oct. 31, 1861 ★ Stephenson, J.L.--Private July 17, 1861. Appears last on roll for Oct. 31, 1861 ★ Streetman, J.N.--Private Sept. 17, 1861. Surrendered, Appomattox, Va. Apr. 9, 1865 ★ Thornton. Rufus--Private July 17, 1861. Absent, sick, Richmond, Va. Oct. 6-31, 1861. No later record ★ Walton, H.A.--Private July 17, 1861. Discharged, disability, Mar. 28, 1865 ★ Walton, S.O.--Private July 17, 1861. Wounded Aug. 1862. Wounded, Wilderness, Va. and sent to hospital May 6, 1864. No later record ★ Watts, R.F.--Private July 17, 1861. Discharged, disability, Nov. 12, 1861. Enlisted as a private, Co. G, 46th Regt. Ga. Inf. Mar. 4, 1862. On detached service, Signal Corps, Charleston, S.C. 1863 - Aug. 1864. Surrendered, Greensboro, N.C. Apr. 26, 1865 ★ Weathersby, A.--Private July 17, 1861. Paid for period Feb. 21 - May 31, 1862, Richmond, Va. June 23, 1862. No later record ★ Weathington, Julius (or Worthington)--Private July 17, 1861. Absent, sick, sent to Mt. Jackson Oct. 6, 1861. Admitted to Chimborazo Hospital #4, Richmond, Va. Aug. 12, 1862. Died, bronchitis, Aug. 18, 1862 ★ Weathington, Samuel J. (or Worthington)--Private July 17, 1861. Discharged, disability, Nov. 24, 1861 ★ Webb, W.A.--Private July 17, 1861. Killed, Darbytown Road, Va. Oct. 7, 1864 ★ Wertheimer, Samuel--Private July 17, 1861. Appears last on roll for Oct. 31, 1861 ★ Willett, Norman--Private Sept. 17, 1861. Surrendered, Appomattox, Va. Apr. 9, 1865 ★ Willett, R.S.--Private Sept. 17, 1861. Appears last on roll for Oct. 31, 1861 ★ Wimberly, J.S.--Private July 17, 1861. Sent to Mt. Jackson Oct. 6, 1861. No later record.

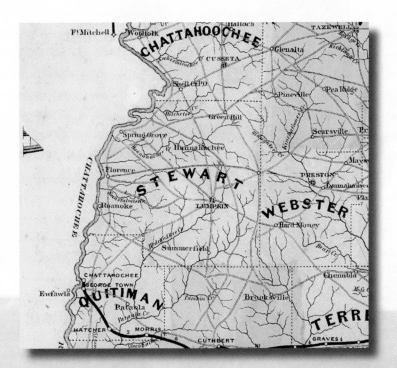

CONCLUSION

S O "TAPS" SOUNDED FOR THE CONFEDERACY, AND THE MEN BEGAN COMING HOME, BACK TO THE MOUNTAINS OF NORTH GEORGIA, TO THE RAVAGED PLANTATIONS OF THE PIEDMONT PLATEAU AND THE SAND HILLS; THROUGHOUT THE IMPOVERISHED STATE, THE SURVIVORS RETURNED TO TRY TO REBUILD LIVES AND BEGIN ANEW. BUT THEY WOULD NEVER BE THE SAME. They brought with them memories they could never completely share, except with each other. This band of brothers had witnessed unspeakable devastation of life and property, and carried grief that men cannot express. They were now, and would be forever, Americans. The land was wounded, but not mortally; it would survive to become the most prosperous nation on earth.

It has been said that the South is defined not by its geography, but by its history. The Civil War was certainly the major defining experience in the South's history, marking its people as the only Americans ever to lose a war and endure an occupation. Forty percent of the South's young men died or were seriously wounded in the war; in sparsely populated Georgia, this was of major consequence.

The men of the 2nd Georgia Infantry Regiment returned, leaving fallen comrades buried far away from home and family. Of the returning soldiers, many were injured and maimed. But they came home and did what all good men do when war is over: they went to work to restore their homes, their farms, their businesses, their relationships with friends and family. In a word, they started over. Their names would be recorded in history books, and live not only in the state's archives, but in their descendants' lives as the state of Georgia blossomed into the Empire State of the South. War may have broken the back of the South; it did not break its spirit. A Southern soldier at the end of the war expressed it this way: "The God of battles was against us, and we were defeated, but not dishonored or disgraced. We returned to homes in ruin, our fortunes gone and nothing left but honor, pluck and energy." The South rose from the ashes of war and these men were a part of that rising.

I believe there is today, because of the war, a broader and deeper patriotism in all Americans; that patriotism throbs the heart and pulses the being as ardently of the South Carolinian as of the Massachusetts Puritan; that the Liberty Bell, even now, as I write, on its Southern pilgrimage, will be as reverently received and as devotedly loved in Atlanta and Charleston as in Philadelphia and Boston. And to stimulate and evolve this noble sentiment all the more, what we need is the resumption of fraternity, the hearty restoration and cordial cultivation of neighborly, brotherly relations, faith in Jehovah, and respect for each other; and God grant that the happy vision that delighted the soul of the sweet singer of Israel may rest like a benediction upon the North and the South, upon the Blue and the Gray.

"From Manassas To Appomattox" General James Longstreet CSA

My Hero
1885

I don't recall how old I was,
But I was very small,
My father seemed so big and strong,
He was almost six feet tall.

He was going to a reunion,
It was an important day.
Because he wore his cap with tassels,
His sword, and uniform of gray.

They talked of battles lost and won,
Of hardships great and small.
I sat very still and listened
But I recall it all.

"Oh weren't you afraid father?" I asked.
"I am sure that I would be."
He looked down at me in surprise.
"No daughter, you see, I fought with Lee!"

(by Virginia Lawton Harper Hay, daughter of Henry Clay
Harper. Written in 1885 while a young girl.)

EPILOGUE

Jackson Elliott Cox,
Second Lieutenant,
Company D, First Battalion,
Third Marine Division,
US Marine Corps

I never met Jack Cox nor ever knew of our relationship as cousins.* I first met Jack through his brother Sidney Cox and their mother, Emily Elliott Cox, while researching and compiling this book. Our meeting established a reconnection of our common ancestry which I cherish to this day. Jack and I were at the same places at the same time in Viet Nam. I did not know that when I left for home I was leaving Jack behind.

In the truest sense though, Jack was not left behind at all. Our country has established a special place at the Vietnam War Memorial. Our family, friends, and indeed, all Americans, have a special place in our hearts for Jack and all of his comrades in arms.

And so, Jack, I tell you that you were a great American and we as citizens of Burke County, the State of Georgia, and the United States of America, love and miss you very much.

God Bless America.

F. Mikell Harper

Jack's great grandmother was Maria Harper Dent, wife of Dr. John M. Dent of Waynesboro, and sister of Henry Clay Harper and James E. Harper.

Located in Waynesboro Presbyterian Church, Waynesboro, Georgia

THE SANCTUARY CROSS
IN MEMORY OF
JACKSON ELLIOTT COX
LIEUTENANT, UNITED STATES MARINE CORPS
TO HIS FRIENDS HE GAVE HIS LOVE
TO HIS COUNTRY - HIS LIFE
1941 - 1967

References

There have been tens of thousands of books, articles, periodicals and other written material concerning the Civil War. The below listed references have been most useful in the preparation of this book and are recommended for use in further study of the Civil War in general, and The 15th Toombs and Bunning's Brigade comprised of The 2nd, 15th,17th and 20th Georgia Infantry Regiments in particular.

The muster rolls contained herein have their origin in Lillian Henderson's monumental work entitled Roster of the Confederate Soldiers of Georgia. Corrections, additions, deletions and other supplemental entries have occurred over time and circumstance. The Muster Rolls of Civil War units in this book continue to be a work in progress and the correction of errors found here should be entered as addenda to these Muster Rolls. Indeed, corrections were made and entered in the service records of Henry Clay Harper and James E. Harper prior to the preparation of this book.

1. Blount, Lucy A. (December 1924). The Burke Sharpshooters. The Confederate Veteran Magazine, XXIV (Dave Dameron, 1997) (James M. McPherson, 2002) (Mark Nesbit, 2002), 464-466.

2. Catton, Bruce (1982). The American Picture History of The Civil War (Richard M. Ketchum, Ed.). New York: American Heritage/Bonanza Books.

3. Corley, F. F. (1995). Confederate City. Spartanburg, SC: The Reprint Company. (Original work published 1960)

4. Dameron, Dave (John Rigdon, 2000) (Drew J. Kendall, 2002) (Tom Elmore, 2002). (1997). Benning's Brigade. Spartanburg, SC: The Reprint Company.

5. Denny, Robert E (1992). The Civil War Years. Sterling Publishing Co. New York, N.Y.

6. Elmore, Tom (2002, February). South Carolina Showdown. Civil War Times Illustrated, 44-55.

7. Gottfried, Bradley M. (2002). Brigades of Gettysburg. Cambridge, MA: Da Capo Press.

8. Hamilton, Posey (1924, February). Incidents of the Fighting at Aiken S. C. The Confederate Veteran Magazine, XXXII, 58-59.

9. Harper, James E. (1864-1865). James E. Harper Diary. Unpublished manuscript.

10. Hill House, A. (1985). A History of Burke County Georgia (1777-1950). Spartanburg, SC: The Reprint Company.
      Honorary Members of Burke Sharpshooters. (1861, Spring). The True Citizen.

11. Kendall, Drew J. (2002, August). Murder at Malvern Hill. Military History, 41-48.

12. Longstreet, James A.(1991). Manassas to Appomattox. New York, N.Y.: The Mallard Press

13. McPherson, James M. (2002). Crossroads of Freedom. New York: Oxford University Press.

14. Miller, T. M.(1911) The Photographic History of The Civil War (Volumes 1-10) New York, N.Y. The Review of Reviews Co.

15. Miller, W. J., & Pohanka, B. C. (2000). An Illustrated History of the Civil War. Alexandria, VA: Time - Life Books.
      National Archives: Compiled Records Showing Service of Military Units in Confederate Organizations, Microfilm Series M61, Roll 12, 2nd Georgia Infantry

16. Nesbit, Mark (2002). Thirty Five Days to Gettysburg. Harrisburg, PA: Stackpole Books.

17. Rigdon, John (2000). The Fighting Fifteenth. Clearwater, SC: Eastern (Albert M. Hillhouse, 1985) (Bradley M. Gottfried, 2002) (Bruce Catton, 1982) (Miller W. J. & Pohanka, 2000)Digital Resources.

18. Rowland IV, Charles B. (Transcription Ed.) (1863-1864). Journal of Catherine B. Whitehead Rowland, 1. [Special issue]

19. The Burke Sharpshooters. (Spring 1902,). The True Citizen.

20. Tucker, P.T. (2000). Burnside's Bridge (1st ed.). Mechanicsburg, PA: Stackpole Books.

Index